FEARLESS AUTHENTICITY

FEARLESS AUTHENTICITY

LEAD BETTER, SELL MORE, AND SPEAK SENSATIONALLY

JEANNE SPARROW

DIVERSION
BOOKS

Diversion Books
A division of Diversion Publishing Corp.
www.diversionbooks.com

For more information, email info@diversionbooks.com

First Diversion Books Edition: January 2025
Hardcover ISBN: 978-1-635-76972-2
e-ISBN: 978-1-635-76962-3

Cover design by Henry Sene Yee
Design by Neuwirth & Associates, Inc.

Printed in the United States of America
1   3   5   7   9   10   8   6   4   2

Diversion books are available at special discounts for bulk purchases
in the US by corporations, institutions, and other organizations.
For more information, please contact admin@diversionbooks.com.

For Allen & Ethel,

whose generous, nurturing hearts

gave me the very best of the Atlas, Malveaux,

and Sparrow family spirit. And for little Jeanne Marie,

that brave girl inside me who has always managed

a way to keep me true to myself.

CONTENTS

FOREWORD

In 1997, I started a new journey as a host of a morning show. Not just any morning show. Not just any radio station. But the #1 radio station in the city of Chicago at that time and one of the most respected and trendsetting radio brands in the nation—107.5 WGCI. The morning show host is the most important personality on any radio station because they're the moneymaker. I was one of the hottest young comedians in all of America, seen on every TV show from *The Tonight Show* to the one and only *Oprah Winfrey Show*. Yes, I did it all. Then I realized there's more to know about myself and who I needed to become.

When I started morning radio, I thought I knew it all. But then I met my cohost, the one and only Jeanne Sparrow. The lady with the greatest smile in the county of Cook and the city of Chicago. When I showed up at 5:00 a.m. for show-time, guess what happened? Ms. Jeanne schooled me. She told me if you want to be the best at this, you've got to be a better you, and that means you need to be here at 4:00 a.m. Four? Why? Preparation, she said. You just can't show up. You've got to be prepared. As the kids say today, show up with ALL the receipts. You've got to know your product. You must know what you're presenting. When you know more about who you are and what you're doing, you can sell all of this and sell yourself better. You can even sell a smile over the radio. It's all about marketing, baby.

The station paid me millions for my personality. They should have paid Ms. Jeanne even more. Jeanne was young at that time but already had the four Ds: she was Devoted to her craft. And yes, she was Disciplined. I guess even at an early age, she knew what she had to do to become a success and she was already adamant about being the best at what she did. She was also Dedicated to her profession. And most importantly, she was Determined to be a better Jeanne.

Through Jeanne Sparrow's *Fearless Authenticity*, it is now your turn to soak up some knowledge about yourself and become the best version of YOU! If you're following Jeanne, don't worry about where you're going. You'll learn it's not always about being in the fast lane, it's about being on the right road. YOURS. Yes, sometimes you've got to exit to refuel, recharge, refresh, and rest to prep for the entire journey. She will put you on track to do all that. Listen to Jeanne. She's one of the smartest people I've ever met.

Jeanne honors her essence and she loves sharing what she does best. I thank Jeanne for making me a better me. Jeanne was with me when I created my favorite catchphrase: "I love you and there's absolutely nothing you can do about it." You'll be saying the same. About her, *Fearless Authenticity*, and yourself.

And buy the book. She needs the money. 😊

—George Wallace

INTRODUCTION

My journey to *Fearless Authenticity* started young, though I didn't realize exactly what was in motion at the time. See, I believe that each of us is put here to do something in particular, and the closer we are to knowing our value and just being ourselves, the more likely we are to share our gifts the way we were meant to, thus moving humankind forward to a better future. But many of us have what my therapist calls faulty beliefs about ourselves that make us believe we have to do or be something other than that for any number of reasons. And the more we believe those things, the less likely we are to be the people we were created to be and carry out the purposes we were meant for.

My own core faulty beliefs took shape in one of my earliest memories. When I was about four, a nun came to visit. I was sitting in my family living room in all its orange glory, from the sofa to the lamps (what can I say, it was the early seventies and my mama had fabulous taste; it's a color I adore to this day). She wasn't one of the nuns who lived in the convent down the street and who I saw when I went to mass at St. Edward; the nuns who would eventually become my teachers at the school there, like Sister Albertine, who played the piano at church. She and Mama were among the handful of pianists in town, so they were friends and she'd stop by to have coffee and visit.

No, this nun was very different from the sisters at St. Edward. She wore a shorter, more colorful habit on her head, dressed in normal clothes, and sounded different. The main difference with her is that she had come to our house just to visit me. It was fun because the only company I'd ever had before were other kids, mainly my cousins. I was happy because she wanted to talk to me and I didn't have to remember to let my parents talk more to the adults, which I eventually figured was only fair since that's who they had come to visit.

I'm sure she asked lots of questions, but I mainly remember the ones about what I was learning. I was in nursery school (that's what they called daycare in the 1900s) and could read my Little Golden Books (they had gold spines and looked pretty all lined up or stacked). I was also fascinated with globes and could tell her all the continents, which I could tell impressed her. I think my parents were surprised, too. We didn't have a globe at home but there was one at the library, another place I loved. Almost as much as the bookmobile later—because who wouldn't want to be in an air-conditioned van full of books? Anyway, I was feeling proud of myself and pretty important that day. Oh, and I also remember talking to her about adoption and explaining to her that's how my parents got me, of course, which she seemed particularly interested in hearing.

One reason that memory is so important to me now is because I later realized how significant it would be in shaping my world. On the surface, which was all I could comprehend at four, it was about being seen—having my own visitor, someone who was interested in me, asking me questions that I got to answer, and, yeah, showing off a little with what I knew, too. As an adult, most of my life's work in radio and television could be distilled down to those same actions—sharing information with a little razzle-dazzle, song-and-dance routine—only I ask most of the questions now. The twist that took me forever to fully understand (though I perhaps sensed it somehow even then) was the way this meeting and the reason for it represented a future pattern that would come to separate me from my authenticity—where I felt I needed to become what was expected of me, explain myself, justify my existence, and/or perform for others to be loved and accepted. Even if I did enjoy creating the performance.

The other reason this memory holds so much sway over me is the why of it all. This would be the first example of many to come on how wrong I could be with the conclusions I had drawn from the limited knowledge I had. I'll get to the specifics in a moment, but I want you to remember this: We often confuse what we *assume* to be true for what is *actually* true. We start to believe these assumptions so strongly that we never question them. We don't always express them out loud to others, so they can't be corrected either. And once they've taken hold, we build entire belief systems around them that can take us down a path that's completely out of alignment with who we truly are—far away from our authentic selves. And that's a lesson I've had to learn and relearn many times since.

So, back to the nun and the orange living room. Turns out this nun was from Catholic Charities and was the case worker for my adoption. Her home visits were part of finalizing my adoption, even though I'd come to live with my parents when I was several months old. I found out decades later that it took a little while for my birth mother to get my birth father's signature on the adoption papers, plus the process was supervised for quite some time anyway before the adoption could be final.

And that lesson around drawing conclusions? Well, a few years later, one of my aunts gained some weight and everybody was talking about her being pregnant and having a baby. I had questions—normal for the observant, inquisitive (nosy!) kid I was—I asked what *pregnant* was, when she and my uncle were going to pick out their baby, and why did she have to get a big tummy just to do that? See, I don't *ever* remember any moment when my parents actually told me I was adopted. I guess they must have at some point, but all I knew was that *adopted* was the word for how we became a family—they chose me and that was it. So, I naturally (to me) thought that's how all families came to be. That every kid was chosen at some baby store somewhere and nuns came to visit them later and ask questions—about their shopping experience, I guess.

So, on top of the usual tap dancing for an age-appropriate way to talk about sex and how babies are really made, my parents were in the probably unenviable position of having to also correct my misunderstanding *and* explain to me that adoption is an alternative way for parents to have children. And they thought I had questions before?! There went my first conclusion, blown out of the water. Then I started thinking again. And the next conclusion I came to was that no matter how much my parents and family loved me now, they might change their minds like the other mommy and daddy did, so I'd better do my best to earn that love. And I kept on drawing conclusions from that moment forward. Some of them correct, some of them, not so much . . . but all with lifelong consequences that led me to *Fearless Authenticity*.

And that, my dear friend, is what this book is all about. How I got to my *Fearless Authenticity*, finally saw and understood my value, and turned what I learned along the way into a process that you can use to find your own *Fearless Authenticity* and make the most of it in your own life and work.

The journey to *Fearless Authenticity* required me to challenge and set down many of those faulty beliefs I held. As you begin to cultivate your own *Fearless Authenticity*, you will have to do the same. Many of us have lost sight of the people we are meant to be in a functional way. We wanted to belong, be loved, feel accepted, or achieve success in life, either the way we define it or, more likely, the way others do, and in the process, we abandon our true selves. Many of us have experienced that—junior high / middle school anybody? I think most of us who experienced feeling as if we were not valued or seen would do anything to *not* feel that way. So, we end up changing something about ourselves or pretending to be somebody we're not, just to fit in. We decide to get some degree or training so we could have some particular job or career to feel accomplished, useful, or productive. The more we make choices like that, the less happy and fulfilled we are as we go on in life. We keep doing the same thing and expect it to finally pay off, only to wake up one day and wonder how we got here.

If you've ever been in any of those places and done any of those things, this book is for you. I have found in my trainings and teaching that my process is helpful for navigating the work transitions of life—moving from school to a job, taking on a new type of position, looking for a promotion, starting a side hustle or business, finding a second career. The process also applies in all the life changes that accompany those transitions—at any age because, as my therapist has also reminded me, it is never too late to heal, change, and grow.

I hope you'll see yourself in the stories I share and know you're not alone in your journey. Because I see it everywhere in my work and hear it in stories from my colleagues and friends in every industry . . . in K–12 and higher education, in my own classes I teach at Northwestern University, with my younger media colleagues, in the music industry, when I'm consulting in corporate environments—literally everywhere! It seems that we have made less time and not created the space in life for this kind of growth. It has all been shortchanged for some temporary gain—whether that's efficiency, cutting costs, or saving time. Yet somehow, we're all still supposed to figure out who we are and what we're meant to do all on our own.

I also want to be clear about what *Fearless Authenticity* is not. Authenticity at work, especially in leadership development, has been a trending topic and a quality of executive presence that has grown in importance in the last decade or so, but especially since the pandemic and the subsequent shift in our priorities with and resulting from the trauma of quarantine lockdowns. Since then, in work culture reporting and writing, there have been as many arguments for as against "bringing your full self" to work. *Fearless Authenticity*, as I define and describe it here, is so much more than that surface-level expression. Certainly, there are parts of what I'll present here that apply similarly, but by and large, *Fearless Authenticity* as a whole is about a development process that is primarily *for yourself.* It is meant to uncover your value—the raw materials you came here with, combined with how they were shaped by and through what you've chosen and experienced on this planet—so you can apply it in whatever way you choose to execute your mission. It doesn't matter what you actually share with others about that knowledge or experience—you can be as vulnerable or as protected as you deem best and safest. It only matters that *you* know your *Fearless Authenticity* and act accordingly.

This may feel a bit counterintuitive from its name, but *Fearless Authenticity* is also not about exceptionalism or individualism in the way it's commonly expressed. Yes, it is about understanding how each of us is special as an individual. But for me, it's in that very understanding that we can see and value how others are special as well. No one can do everything well. Nor should we even try. I don't even want to. I'm so happy to let others shine in the way they're meant to—even if they do something similar to me. If each of us can get to that point and only do what we're supposed to do, then we get to become the highest expression of that thing . . . and then each of us becomes a distinct piece in this grand puzzle that fits together perfectly as part of a whole. Thus, becoming clearer about who we are as individuals helps us see how to build a stronger, healthier, and more durable community with others.

Fearless Authenticity is also how we find our true successes in life. Not only is it far easier to be ourselves than to imitate another, but when we know who we are and what we can create or accomplish, we can communicate our value to others more clearly. That helps us find our people, the places where we fit, and do our best work. With each success that leads to, we gain more solid confidence that's rooted in our accomplishments and growth, instead of through cheap comparisons and unhealthy competition. Getting rid of the shaky things that prop us up also helps us find a better vantage point from which to see and connect with others through their needs and their gifts, perhaps even encourage them in their development and growth. All that allows us to partner and team up better with others, because we rarely make progress alone.

No matter where you are in your journey, I hope this book becomes a tool to help you see and become more yourself and make the most of your talents, skills, and gifts—to make up for all those times when you couldn't see them and didn't have anyone to help you find them. I also hope it helps you zoom out and see how everything is connected, because when we each find our own way, we give others permission to do the same. Finding and using your *Fearless Authenticity*, even though it is a very personal journey, brings you closer to the collective and pushes our momentum forward in community, together. Choosing to take this journey is how you do your part to create a better, more satisfying, and authentic world.

PART I

—————

AUTHENTIC POWER

CHAPTER 1

Be Brave, Be Free, Be You

BE BRAVE

Everybody's mama told them these same eight words on the first day of school: "*Baby, just be yourself and you'll make friends.*" Of course, she was right (mamas always are), but she didn't tell me *how* to do it. To be fair, even if she had explained it to me, it probably wouldn't have done much good. It sounds so simple to say *just be yourself*, but it's easier said than done, at any age. That's what this book is all about—giving you a process to find your way to the beauty of your *Fearless Authenticity*, whether it's for the first time or getting back what you've lost of it along your way in life.

If you're reading this, chances are you've found the deceptively simple advice to *just be yourself* challenging in some way. You're not alone in that experience. There are a lot of reasons that's true for all of us and, sometimes, we're not even aware of what these reasons are. For me, it was hard to be fearless and express my most authentic self because of who I am and how I came to be.

I'm adopted, which I've always known. It was never a secret. My parents wanted me to know the truth of who I was and that I was chosen, wanted, and very loved. When I was young, that was all I knew. I felt all those things deep in my bones. But as I got older, I started putting things together. I realized that to be chosen in this way, I also had to be given away.

When I realized this truth, I also realized that to be loved and wanted by my family meant another family had to let me go. Even if it was for the best, even if there were the best intentions behind that decision, what it said to me was that I wasn't wanted somewhere, that people who were supposed to love and protect me had chosen not to do that. They rejected me for some reason. In my head, that meant something was wrong with me and that I had to prove myself worthy to even be here, to be loved.

As an adoptee, I always felt like I slipped in through the back door. That if I didn't do things well and show why I should be here, then I wasn't actually worth the effort to anyone. If I didn't get good grades, wasn't good company or entertaining, I wasn't living up to my end of the bargain to justify why I deserved to stay here. That logic convinced me that if the people who were supposed to take care of me decided they couldn't, then whoever took over for them was doing me a favor. I looked at everything with that twisted logic. It made me strive for perfection every day because, if I was perfect, then they had no reason not to love me. I would, of course, get something wrong, but that didn't stop me from playing back conversations and events in my head

4

to make sure I didn't do "something wrong" again. That mindset also led me to apologize for everything when I was younger, whether it was my fault or not. I always told myself I should have known better, done better. I was in essence always walking on eggshells that I created for myself. Back then, I thought it was normal to do all that and feel that way all the time. And when I feel insecure now, I have to consciously choose not to go back to that same behavior, because no matter how damaging it was, it's still familiar and even reassuring.

That's how I started down the slippery slope of not always being fearless or authentic. When you're always trying to validate yourself and show everyone that you deserve a place in this world, you end up saying or doing things to toe some imaginary line that someone else set, instead of toeing the line you know is true and right for you.

That slide slowed down when I finally found a label for what I'd been missing. To name a thing is to know a thing, right? When I was able to name *Fearless Authenticity*, life and work made more sense. I saw what my value was, what I had to offer the world and others, and stopped trying to explain or justify what I wanted, needed, and was good at when it wasn't ever going to make sense to them. I stepped into the power of my own unique experience and skills without apology. I was unequivocally *not* sorry.

At that point, with all the advice I'd gotten and used, everything I'd learned so far, my experience of how I came to be clicked into place. I *did* have something to offer—that show-offy little girl who thought she always had the answers finally had some. I knew my value and ability to tell stories well, both mine and others', and do it in a way that connects

5

with audiences of all kinds for different uses—leadership, sales/marketing, speaking, and more. And I knew I could show others how to do the same to help them reach their goals, especially in their work. Knowing that helped me think bigger about the work I was already doing when I started my business. Until then, I had limited myself to what I knew—media coaching—never realizing the full value, application, and potential for all my skills. So, I stopped thinking small and put deliberate intention into delivering the full impact of what I was already offering.

By naming *Fearless Authenticity* and clearly defining the way I approach it, I began to fully see the value in myself. (I'll help you find your value in chapter 2.) I've always seen my value through my work, because what I've done for a living has mostly been an extension of how I've always justified my presence. If someone couldn't see my value, I would try my best to convince them and, sometimes, I succeeded. So exhausting and unnecessary. The shift away from that didn't happen overnight, though. (I'm still working on it. For instance, writing this book has been the biggest challenge and commitment of my life—and I often felt like the biggest fraud doing it, even though I was so excited about it. That voice that draws faulty conclusions would ask me: "*Who do you think you are to write an entire book? You can write a speech or a bit but that's it.*" But I shut that voice down with what's next.)

When I first named *Fearless Authenticity*, I also created a mantra to keep me focused and grounded in it: *Be Brave, Be Free, Be You. Be Brave* is first because it makes the other two possible. Taking a chance means *Being Brave*—fearless even. Being fearless doesn't mean having no fear; it means you acknowledge whatever you're afraid of and move forward anyway. And putting your authentic self and talents out there into the world without a mask takes courage. *Be Free* because to fully step into your own power, you need to first throw away all the expectations, judgments, and roles that others (and you) have put on you and that you've felt obligated to fulfill. These burdens may even be weighing you down or holding you back. Once you're free of all that, you can choose what you accept, ask for, and accomplish on your terms (which is also scary, so please refer back to *Be Brave* as needed). And *Be You* because you are the gift. You know your value, worth, and gifts and can let others know about them and share them as you see fit. When you can take steps every day to *Be Brave, Be Free, Be You*, then you're walking on your path to *Fearless Authenticity*.

I want to be crystal clear that *Fearless Authenticity* is for *you*. It's not for other people, even if you use it to sell yourself to others in order to get what you want and need. It's really about you knowing and making that connection inside yourself, *for yourself*. It's a knowing that goes so deep that you never ask if you "deserve it," because you do. You know and believe without question that you have whatever you need inside you. Because if you're questioning it or always looking for external validation or whatever your struggle is (and we all have them), nobody can convince you otherwise, and you certainly won't be able to convince anybody else. Unless . . . unless you luck out, somebody sees your potential, and decides to give you a shot. However, making the most of that takes you right back to the first thing—you've got to believe in yourself!

The purpose of *Be Brave* is to push through fear to create and solidify belief in yourself. It can be daunting to keep the faith when you know you're up against big odds—and others' doubts. That's why I'm in awe of my friend and acclaimed Chicago mystery author Tracy Clark's unwavering faith in herself and her abilities. She knew practically from the womb that she wanted to be a writer.

"I took every class and learned everything," she said. "I knew I had that foundation. And, of course, I'm stubborn as all get-out. I had a choice: I can either keep going and see how far I could go with it and hopefully get where I needed to go. Or I could stop and then I would sort of regret that, because I knew this was me. This is what I wanted to do."

She now has two award-winning crime series set in Chicago, each featuring a doggedly determined Black female detective. However, it took twenty years, a three-inch-thick file of rejection letters, and an unrelenting desire to get there.

"You have to believe in what you're doing," she told me. "You have to have stick-to-itiveness. . . . You have to have this sort of internal fire that stays bright all the time. And whether people come at you with hoses, trying to put that fire out, it doesn't work because . . . you know what you're about at that point. There's no secret formula to it. You just have to keep on going."

Tracy's right—there is no secret formula. I think we all wish there was one—some magical potion that could make our dreams come true. That's why we love and believe in fairy tales so much. And yet, those stories of our childhood also told some unavoidable truths of life. Even Cinderella knew that you can't skip the work. And the work takes *Being Brave* . . . brave enough to do what's necessary to honor your authentic self and gifts. As long as you are making an effort to move forward and examining how things are working for you, you're on a journey to becoming yourself or, more accurately, remembering yourself. I love how author Emily McDowell summed it up:

"Finding yourself is not really how it works. You aren't a ten-dollar bill in last winter's coat pocket. You are also not lost. Your true self is right there, buried under cultural conditioning, other people's opinions, and inaccurate conclusions you drew as a kid that became your beliefs about who you are. Finding yourself is actually returning to yourself. An unlearning, an excavation, a remembering of how you were before the world got its hands on you."

Clients often ask me, "How do I know who I am?" I find this question comes up at different stages in people's lives, usually during some change in life. One of those junctions is when someone has children who are ready to leave the nest. Parents will wonder: "Wait, now, who am I? Who am I separate from being this person's mother or father? They've turned into a grown human and I've done my job. So, who am I *now*?" They've become lost in their parental duties, just like we lose ourselves in our jobs or our other relationships.

But even when we get lost, we're always answering that "Who am I?" question in a way that's relevant for the moment. *Be Brave* enough to be intentional about it. When you find yourself in one of those transitional times, wondering who you are, look for the clues to who you were and what you were doing right before the transition began, because that's how you made it to this point. Then also look to who you want to be and what you want to do in the next phase after the transition. Let's say the transition is a promotion or moving on to a better job with more responsibilities—who were you and what did you do in your last position that led to this new opportunity? How did you relate to your coworkers? How was your approach to your work unique? Then look into your future and decide how you want to answer those same questions when you move on from this new position. Who we are is always evident in the way we move through life, trying to do our best: at work, with family, and by/for ourselves. You are already on your *Fearless Authenticity* journey; you're on your way to becoming that and doing the thing you were put here to do, whether or not you know it or are doing it intentionally.

We get so confused and mentally separated from our authenticity and purpose because we believe what society tells us about the things *it* wants from us instead of what we want for ourselves. And other people have individual expectations that tell us the things *they* want from us. There's nothing wrong with any of that on the surface. The problem happens when our interpretations of all that get twisted into faulty beliefs about ourselves, and we change to fit those expectations in a way that is better for them than it is for us. We confuse what we think about ourselves and what we need to be based on what other people want and need, and that blocks our vision of who we truly are. But we were always here. This *Fearless Authenticity* journey is about *Being Brave* enough to stand up to those faulty beliefs and get back to ourselves.

BE FREE

So, how do we find our way back?

A. You're already doing it.

B. You can make it more transparent and intentional by actually saying, "Wait a minute! I'm reclaiming this territory that other people have encroached on." That means breaking away from fulfilling roles others have defined for you, releasing yourself from others' expectations that don't align with yours, and liberating yourself from others' judgments, especially those that keep you from what you know is right for you. *Being Free* is choosing all those things for yourself as you see it—and leaving all the judgment, especially of yourself, behind. When you choose to *Be Free*, it looks a lot like having healthy boundaries. Think of it this way—you've got people on your lawn like it's a picnic, taking up *your* space with *their* shit. Now it's time for you to kick them out so you can have your own picnic the way you want.

This need to stake a claim for freedom happens to all of us, whether we had a supportive upbringing or one that was lacking. Renowned spoken word artist Malik Yusef grew up on Chicago's South Side, and his creative spirit was ignored as he struggled with dyslexia while his three brothers' talents were nurtured.

"The majority of the residential resources went to my brothers," he said. "I was not poured into . . . I wasn't paid attention to, and things you don't pay attention to, you don't edify . . . but I always had it in me. I sought freedom [through] creation. I didn't need tools around me. I could create in my mind."

11

And create he did, as a poet, rapper, writer, composer, director, deejay, activist, and producer, winning eight Grammys, several Emmys, a Tony Award, and a Peabody Award, while directing and starring in multiple movies, TV shows, and documentaries. All that to say, he finally convinced himself that his art was worth sharing, and he overcame other people's limited expectations for him.

"I look at everything as an opportunity, because when you're trying to escape a situation, you have to kind of investigate all thoroughfares. And that's how it came . . . I love the freedom it [art and creativity] provides."

I was the same way, even though I had a very different upbringing filled with support and love. Part of the reason I struggled with my writing is that I didn't think I had a story worth sharing before I started writing this book. But I've come to realize *we all have a story to tell.* You don't know what's unusual about your story, because it's your story and you've been living with it, so that's what you know. If you compare it to what you see on TV—well, that's not real, even if it's presented as "reality." And if you compare it to other people's lives, you only know what they've told you and that's rarely the whole story. Or if you compare it to what you see on Instagram or any social media platform, well, I think you know that's just what they want to show you.

The person I present to the world is always a real piece of me. But it's taken me into my fifties to be that whole person most of the time. My journey is ongoing, and I'll continue to be on it because I'll continue to change, learn new things, even with my adoption story. I dealt with it in my twenties in therapy, healing those first layers after my mama died. But as I got older and experienced more, like the loss of my father and facing my birth mother with some tough questions, I realized that trauma was affecting me in new ways and had new things to teach me about myself, which deepened my understanding of *Fearless Authenticity* and how I share it. I thought that all I had to share was as simple as my origin story. I found that it is—and it isn't. It's so much more.

In a similar way, as you grow in your gifts, you're going to move closer to the essence of what they're supposed to be about and how you're supposed to use them in that moment. So, get comfortable with change and uncertainty. Easier said than done, I know. What you do well at one point in your life, you will do better later. Or, what you thought you had dealt with already, may come back to teach you something new. *Being Free* means being unencumbered or unattached to how things have been, so you can recognize when things begin to change and welcome that instead of resisting it. Change is inevitable if you want to grow—you can't have one without the other. To get success or whatever you want, you have to make space for it. I'm sharing this with you now so you can start looking for some of these things in your own life as we move through these chapters.

BE YOU

This is where it starts for you in your *Fearless Authenticity* journey. Just look at who you are. Look at where you came from. Interrogate yourself and your beliefs. Why do you believe what you do about yourself, your abilities, work, money, success, love, the world, and the way it works? What do you believe is possible or impossible, and who first told you that? You owe it to yourself to question everything. You may find, as I did, that all you believe to be true may not actually be so—and it could be even better. We all have an origin story; it's what guides us through life, even if it's just playing in the background. That story and how it came to be helps us understand where we belong, shows us we are enough, and teaches us how to be fearlessly ourselves and come out on top.

Isn't that what we all want? To fit in; to find our community and be successful? The pandemic sabotaged our ability to feel connected; to feel like we're a part of something besides fear and chaos; it infringed on our capacity to be our best, most honest, true, and unique selves. We were so busy trying to stay safe and healthy, we forgot who we really are, what we really want, and how to express that.

While COVID made me question some of my life choices, I wasn't completely out of my element. I've had to adapt my whole career—from a prospective agent telling me I'd never earn as much as a white man, to getting fired for insubordination from my first job as a radio copywriter, to quitting a good reporting job because I had accomplished all I wanted to in that job and was frankly bored, to getting fired again from a TV job I loved—but all that catapulted me into starting my own business, and here we are.

After each of those turning points, I called my daddy (I'm a daddy's girl, if I'm being authentic), and he would always say: "Jeanne, people are gonna do what they do, but that has nothing to do with you. You can't change that. The only thing you can do is just keep doing what you've been doing—being yourself and showing up every day."

That's *Fearless Authenticity* in a nutshell from my daddy. He lived *Fearless Authenticity* every day.

More on him in a bit. First, let's focus on you. How do you show up every day as yourself in your world? And if you don't have a clue, don't feel bad. Let me tell you about a client who was struggling to find her true self and how we worked together to realize her full potential.

Rachel was referred to me by her boss, an alum of the MSc (master of science) program where I teach at Northwestern University. He asked me to coach her for a new leadership role, because he said she always seemed hesitant or scared to speak up.

"But when she does," he said, "when she shares her opinion, it's amazing and it really helps me to think about what it is that I need to do."

His goal was to elevate her to a chief of staff role. At that point, she was an executive assistant but definitely doing higher level work already.

When I talked with Rachel, she said she felt like everybody was so much more experienced than she.

"Of course they are," I said. "They're executives. They've gotten to that point. But you've actually done the work that your organization does; you want to help young people who are caught up in the system or have mental health issues and create a safe space for them—that's why you're working here. How many of the people who run the organization have done that work? You bring a whole different perspective."

After we had worked together for a while, she realized what she had to offer to people who she thought were far more successful than she, people she was intimidated by, and she understood what she had to do.

"I just need to be me," she said, "and see where I fit into this organization."

I had a similar challenge when I first started in radio. And let me tell you, finding my authentic self behind a microphone wasn't easy at first. Remember that perfection thing I thought I needed as a kid? That kicked in, and I tried to be word perfect on the air. The pursuit of perfection has been something I've been trying to unlearn for most of my adulthood. I thought that being perfect would solve any shortcomings, when, in reality, even if perfect were possible, it still wouldn't be perfect for somebody else. Everyone has their own version of perfect.

One of my first radio bosses told me, "You need to loosen up a little bit and be more like the woman I hear when I talk to you in person." He told me that if I was going to have staying power, listeners needed to remember me. And the only way that would happen was if they got to know the real me—my perspective, my opinions, my personality, my knowledge—not just some perfect-sounding or sexy voice coming through their speakers that could be switched with any other voice that sounded the same. He gave me a choice and I made it because I wanted to last.

I learned pretty quickly that even if I didn't feel comfortable sharing *all* of me, some version of my real self had to show up and share my unique perspective. When I got my first regular on-air radio gig in Chicago, I was doing traffic reports for morning and afternoon shows. For the first few months, I was scared to death that one of the hosts would ask for my opinion because I didn't want to say anything that would offend anybody or get me in trouble. Then I got paired with Danny Bonaduce (child star on *The Partridge Family*, lots of scandals and drugs, but he's good now) on a talk station and all that perfection *had* to go out the window.

I know, it sounds crazy and impossible now, but it ended up being exactly what I needed to come into my own. I think the programmers on that station were trying to create a dynamic like that between Howard Stern and Robin Quivers—you know, pair the proper, educated Black girl with the loud shock jock, white guy and let the shenanigans ensue. Danny may have been walking on the edge, but like Howard, he's super-smart, funny, and quick, so he was easy to talk to and a challenge for me at the same time, because I had to match that energy. Unlike me, he wasn't worried about being perfect. Far from it. He just wanted to win.

It was the first time doing talk radio for both of us, so we had a lot to learn about the format—and about working with each other. We had a great producer who helped us figure out our rhythm and dynamic. My job/role quickly became "voice of reason" and "keeping Danny in line." This worked fine for me, since in comparison to his, my life was very tame. I couldn't believe some of the stuff that would fly out of his mouth. He was always pushing the envelope with everything, including crazy questions about my personal life. One day, he pushed a little too far and I let him have it on-air—damn near cursed him out and was just shy of breaking all the FCC rules. The phones lit up. He loved it and told me he knew I had it in me and was waiting (and poking and prodding) for that side of me to show up on-air. What surprised me the most was the listener response. It tickled them and they all wondered how I let him get away with so much before checking him.

That's when I learned from firsthand experience that connecting with an audience is mainly about sharing myself and the lens through which I interpret things. It doesn't really matter how what I say comes out, as long as it's real. The people out there who get me are *my* audience, even when I'm sharing them with others. From that moment on, I wasn't scared to say what I had to say or share something about myself (to an extent—I was far from fearless or fully authentic but I was on the path). That audience connection I made then and learned how to maintain has always been important in the media business, but now, more people have realized it is important for everyone, no matter what you do.

The reality is, if you're just some cookie-cutter version of the title you have or job you hold, then that's not really about you. You're not bringing anything new to the conversation. But if you can bring *all* of who you are, your full authentic self—all the different identities, qualities, background, and experiences you've had—if you can say, "This is what I think and that's where I stand in that," then you just made a big step forward for yourself *and* made the world a better place, too.

Part of bringing your whole self to a situation is also knowing when it's time to go. When I walked away from a full-time TV job in Chicago, some people questioned my sanity. They couldn't understand why I would give up something others would give anything to have. But I knew in my head and heart that I needed to try something new. I kept thinking, *This can't be all there is.* So, I left NBC and freelanced until I finally got my dream job hosting my own TV show on WCIU-TV.

In our professional lives, we're often waiting for somebody to offer us what we want. We want people to read our mind. Instead, you have to be bold enough, you have to be brave enough to trust that you know what is right for you—not what others think is right—and take the leap.

I have been paid to be fearless so many times—stood on stages in front of thousands of people, risked making a fool of myself trying something new like riding an elephant at the circus, swinging from a trapeze in a theater, or playing with a snake for a reptile show and somehow letting it get into my shirt on live television (and yes, there's video that you may be able to google). Don't get me wrong—I was scared but I still showed up. There were a few things I turned down because it didn't feel comfortable to me (pinup photos—I know, go figure), but it's my nature to try new things, so whether I was intentional and asked to do it (elephant in the circus), was offered or challenged to do it (trapeze), or it just happened on its own (snake in my shirt), I realized that I had to keep doing me, trusting my gut, and being true to myself. And you know what? It's worked out. Thirty-some years later, I'm still here. I found my people who built on that foundation along the way (or they found me) and I did my best to sidestep those who wanted to tear it down. I've gone from radio to television and back to radio again. I've told so many amazing stories, helped lots of people, met all kinds of celebrities, and won seven Emmy Awards.

As I did all that, people would ask me to speak, consult, coach, and I was eager to share my experience, all while I was still on my way to finding what it really meant to be *Fearlessly Authentic* for me. I feel like the more you know about yourself and the more you can share about yourself to the point that you're comfortable, the more value you can bring to others (we'll dig into finding your value in the next chapter).

You need to be able to tell people your worth and how they can benefit by telling your story. When you are very clear about what you do, how it's good for other people, and why you love it—that will be communicated in every single thing you do, even if you *never* say one actual word about it. When you are clear, your whole body communicates it, and you radiate the *Fearless Authenticity* of being comfortably, undeniably you.

That's what I learned from my daddy, whose fearlessly authentic self continued to show up even after his dementia worsened in early 2020 and I had to move him into a nursing home in our hometown at age eighty-two.

I was filled with dread, but he settled right in. A couple weeks later, my cousin, who lives near the nursing home, called. She said, "Girl, I just came back from seeing your daddy."

It was barbershop day in the home and my dad was waiting with the other men for it to open. When the announcement was made, she said one guy in a wheelchair was struggling a bit so my dad flipped up the brakes on his chair and wheeled him down the hall. "It was like your dad was in a parade, waving and smiling at the people in the hall. He was a superstar; he found his purpose for being there."

I was crying tears of joy, because in that moment I knew my dad was in the right place, and he was serving his audience with aplomb.

Daddy's irrepressible charm even showed up in the emergency room when he caught COVID-19 a few months later. His nurse told me when I called, "He's doing great, and surely I don't have to tell you, but he is just the sweetest, nicest man."

I was a bit surprised, but I really shouldn't have been. Daddy was just working his magic again. He'd found a way to work the room, even in the ER. Really, Daddy? It was so on point, so on brand, so fearlessly, authentically Spro (my dad's nickname).

That was the last time I saw my daddy's magic at work. I lost him a few days later. Though he's gone in body, I know his spirit is with me always.

What I've come to know since his death is that he was teaching me another lesson in his final days. He proved to me that no matter where you are—in a hospital isolation room during a pandemic—and no matter who you are in relation to all those people around you—an elderly patient with dementia—you can *still* make a difference in people's lives, just by being yourself. Your truly beautiful, fearlessly authentic self. You show people who you are, what you have to offer, even when it seems like you have nothing and you need their help.

My father showed me that being your authentic self is the essence and the value of what we are on this planet to accomplish. If my dad can have that kind of impact after dementia had ravaged his brain and while he was struggling to breathe with COVID, that's evidence that *nothing* could erase the most valuable thing about him—*himself*, his fearless, authentic essence that he gave freely to others.

And if he can do that, we all certainly can. No matter what's going on, what we're dealing with, no matter where we are. Our authenticity is already there inside us, waiting to be revealed and fulfill our purpose. We only have to be fearless and share that gift with the world. When we do, the world returns the favor and opens up to us in ways we could have only imagined.

BE BRAVE, BE FREE, BE YOU
AUTHENTICITY ACTION

Questions to ask yourself:

- **Be Brave**—Ask yourself—what can you be brave in doing today? Perhaps in trying something you've been afraid of trying or afraid of failing at?

- **Be Free**—What can you let go of or reveal about yourself that could become an advantage in reaching your goals?

- **Be You**—When have you not shown up as yourself and why?

CHAPTER 2

Uncovering Authenticity, Discovering Value

The pandemic and subsequent years-long quarantine offered people the opportunity to assess the quality of their lives, paying special attention to their employment. They embarked on a journey that I call "Uncovering Authenticity and Discovering Value." They questioned if what they were doing aligned with who they were and what they wanted to put out in the world.

That evaluation led to an unprecedented mass employee exodus in 2021, dubbed the *Great Resignation*. Forty-seven million people quit their jobs that year, according to the US Bureau of Labor Statistics. Departures continued at a record pace in 2022 (50.5 million), along with a new trend—"quiet quitting." Millions of employees were just meeting their job description and not going above and beyond at work. Gallup found that at least 50 percent of the US workforce was made up of quiet quitters.

Let's talk about "quiet quitters" for a minute. I hate that term . . .

We need to look below the surface of the Great Resignation and quiet quitting to understand why people were unhappy with their jobs in the first place. The pandemic was a wake-up call to many who started examining their career choices across industries. The complete global chaos caused by COVID-19 (remote work/school, feelings of isolation, and fear for our lives) influenced what was happening in our heads with regard to our priorities and perspectives. We wanted better engagement, better hours, better pay, and work-life balance. Our exploration of who we are and what we bring to the table provided an opening to realign and recommit to our goals or make new ones.

We can't ignore the pandemic's impact on those who chose to stay in their positions (about eighty-five million), whether working from home, staying in the office, or following a hybrid schedule. Many lost touch with who they were, what they wanted, and how to express either. They felt like rubber balls, bouncing back and forth between in-person and virtual settings. They were worn out from talking to a screen all day.

All of us, whether we left or stayed in our jobs, lost our way at some point. But many of us used that feeling as a launchpad to uncover our authenticity and discover our value. This process of revealing these core elements of ourselves creates the foundation for how we'll define, express, and share our authentic self with others. There's so much power in knowing and specifically stating what you have to offer—what marketers call our *value proposition*—and what you hold dear. Like a company's mission statement and core values, this foundation tells everyone what you stand for, what you do, and what you're worth. It allows us to more fully live and walk in our mantra of *Be You*. As you know, simply by being you, you cultivate your *Fearless Authenticity*.

Sometimes it's not that you need to start from scratch; you just need to remember what you already knew about yourself. A woman I coached who worked in community relations for an energy company was struggling to return to in-person meetings where she had to speak in front of people, but felt out of practice.

"I used to do this all the time," she said. "It used to be second nature to me, and I don't even know how to exercise those muscles anymore."

To help her get back in that rhythm, I had her consider and refocus on her value as an individual (you'll learn how to find yours a little later in this chapter) and how that reflected the company's value to its clients and stakeholders, through her role as its representative. She knew how important it was to meet in person to connect, build trust, and strengthen existing relationships, and how skilled she was at these essential factors in the success of projects that impacted a community's way of life.

At the beginning of the pandemic, she had quickly made the necessary adjustments to maintain those relationships in virtual settings, but when the option of in-person meetings was available again, it was an awkward transition back to the way things used to be. Once she let go of the feeling that she had "lost" her skills for in-person presentations and started practicing to regain that muscle memory, she tapped into her value, found her groove again, and was able to more easily switch between virtual and in-person meetings when representing the company.

Gen Zers were also in a similar predicament because their careers started remotely, giving them few chances to make real connections with coworkers, supervisors, and clients. They led the quiet-quitting trend, having what some call a quarter-life crisis. A quick examination of their lives so far left them feeling underutilized and underdeveloped.

Regardless of age group, the overwhelming question on most everyone's mind was: Based on what I'm seeing outside and how I'm feeling inside—why aren't things matching up? I'd say the mismatch is in value, where you don't clearly know what you have to offer to others, or in purpose, where you haven't discovered what's truly important to you about sharing the gifts you have. Or both. Depending on where you are in life and career, that could look like working harder or for longer hours and getting a higher salary or gaining a better position, but asking yourself why those accomplishments somehow still feel hollow. In this case, you may be offering all the value you have, but if the work doesn't have any meaning to you in fulfilling your purpose, it feels useless. Or it could be wondering why the success you were aiming for always seems just beyond your reach. This situation could be because you're not in a place where you're able to offer your value. Or worse yet, perhaps it just looks like burnout—feeling depleted and unfulfilled, which is probably where you're not using your gifts or making an impact that's meaningful to you.

Any one of those situations and countless other variations could make you wonder, *What am I missing?* I can say with total confidence that once you know your value, and your purpose is aligned with that through your work, you won't ever ask those questions. When you know your reason for being somewhere, the only questions you will ever ask are, "*How can I do more of that?*" and "*What do I need to do to take the next step?*" When you see how you're able to benefit others with the value you bring and match that with the impact you want to make, you start to move differently through life.

Illinois lieutenant governor Juliana Stratton didn't set out to shatter barriers as the first Black woman to serve as a constitutional officer in state history. She shared with me that she always thought it "was more important for me to think about: What are the gifts that I've been created with? What are the things that are in me? And how can I use that wherever I am?"

She used her gifts first to become a lawyer, focusing on juvenile justice and elder law. Those interests led her to start a mediation firm and then move to positions at different government agencies. The first political office she held was on the local school council at Chicago's Kenwood Academy—her alma mater.

"I was just passionate about access to public education," she said. "I didn't look at it from a standpoint of what is the title that I could have or the office that I could hold? I looked at it as what strengths do I have? What do I believe I've been put on this earth to do? What I found is that when you're focused on using your gifts, there will be room made for you . . . whichever space you find yourself in to utilize those gifts . . . I think it is really important for all of us to do an assessment of that. What am I good at?"

A further point she made was to not just focus on what you're good at but to think about "what intrinsically is in me that says, 'If I had to do this every single day, it would feel amazing.'"

For me, the lieutenant governor is the embodiment of *Fearless Authenticity*. She knows the value she brings through her gifts, and she achieves her purpose by using them everywhere and in every way she can. She moves through life with a mission to serve others and enjoys it. This raises the question: What would you do every single day that would bring you fulfillment and offer value to others?

To answer that question, as the lieutenant governor said, you need to know that who you are and what you bring to everything you do, at work and in your personal life, is what makes your contribution special. *Be You*—your perspective, your opinion, your experiences—that is where your value is and what gives you power. Once you know yourself and your worth, you will absolutely add something to the work you do and better serve your audience. My students prove this is true at every level, every term I teach. Most of them are in their first jobs after being undergrads or looking for their first big career opportunity. It can be very challenging at entry-level positions to see how your contribution is special. Sometimes you can focus on your unique value; other times, it's about the effect your work has.

One student whose work involved providing access to resources for young people in underserved communities realized that his own personal struggles with identity and judgment when he was a teen gave him a point of connection that helped him motivate and assist these young people who are made to feel small, if they're ever noticed at all. And when I spoke at a mortgage company, an entry-level worker questioned how there could possibly be any value in her work when all she did was "just push buttons" on home loan applications. I asked her, how did she think a prospective, first-time home buyer would feel if she didn't push those buttons? She immediately saw the big impact she had on a person's life, just by pushing those buttons. We all have to start somewhere, but we're always delivering value.

Before we delve into what your value is and isn't, I want to remind you that we as humans, because of the fact that we're even here, have intrinsic value. Just by the fact that we show up every day. We are here and we have something to offer. Period. In addition, I want to be clear that even though my exercise is based on work, or what we want to do, or the impact we want to have, your value is not solely from your work. Your value is because of who you are, your experiences in what you bring to every situation.

HOW DID I GET HERE?

The reason I use work as an entry point into finding value is because we spend so much of our lives, especially as Americans, working. Our identity is often defined by our work, so I think it's an easy way to see what we spend our time on; and what benefits and value we bring to others through that. (And, if I'm being totally honest, it's how I first connected to my own value in the world; even as a child, how well I did in school and my parents' reactions to my achievements were proof to me that I was a good human being who deserved good things. And, yes, I've been in therapy and since realized that my worthiness is more than my work. Now, back to you.)

Let's start with the product—in this case, you—and look at the work you put into the world:

- Are you doing something you always knew you wanted to do?

- Or did you end up doing something because it's easy for you, you're good at it, enjoy it, or maybe just tolerate it?

- Perhaps you were guided to it by a colleague or family member?

- Did the opportunity fall in your lap or did the environment you grew up in encourage it?

- Have the steps you've taken since you started your career been unintentional or deliberate?

These are good questions to ask yourself if you're experiencing burnout, wondering why your wins feel empty, or you are feeling any sort of disconnect with your work. The answers can help you see where that dissatisfaction is coming from—is it the work itself or what you do or don't get from it? Those are clues that will provide a starting point for the questions at the end of this chapter.

Realize that answering these questions may shake things up a bit and give you a new direction to consider. It's also possible that your discoveries will convince you to stay the course or just do a little fine-tuning. Examining and understanding how you got where you are now and adding intention to what you do next is the prep work to finding the value in what you're doing and deciding if it matches your purpose.

To begin your journey toward uncovering your authenticity and finding your value, think about how these statements apply to your work:

- This is what I do.

- This is what I do well and/or uniquely.

- This is what I'm supposed to be doing with what I do well.

When you walk into a room, what you think of yourself and how you feel about yourself, especially regarding the value that comes from what you do well, walks in with you. That's really what the vibe check—how you read the room and how the room reads you—is all about. Before you ever open your mouth to say anything to anyone, your energy has already introduced you to the room. So, it makes sense to get clear on what your *thing* is and how you think and feel about it.

I want you to consider this fully because, often, we don't think that purposefully about what we do, who we are, or how we move. But the minute we add intentionality to our process, the outcomes we create are charged with a different energy. They become stronger and more impactful—they become more powerful through our focus.

Chinese mystic philosopher Lao Tzu said, "Watch your thoughts, they become your words; watch your words, they become your actions; watch your actions, they become your habits; watch your habits, they become your character; watch your character, it becomes your destiny." That is a very direct route from what you think to where you end up.

Everyone has their favorite morning show or late-night TV host: Maybe you like their interview style or their sense of humor or their view on current events. We make a choice about whom we watch because of that individuality. The same is true for each and every one of you—who you are and what you bring to everything you do, at work, in your personal lives, everything. True diversity comes from diversity of thought. Every one of us is diverse, whether we are in the majority or not. We all have things that we have gone through, whether it's our education, socioeconomic status, home environment, all these things impact how we see life and interpret it. That is where your value is.

Trying to be like everybody else is just going to make you that much more replaceable. If you're a cog in the wheel, then somebody else can be that cog. You stand out depending on how you bring to the table who you are and what your experiences are, particularly in your workplace. If you can share your experience as an immigrant, a member of the LGBTQIA+ community, an autistic person, or somebody for whom English is an additional language, I guarantee you and your particular perspective will add something to the work you do, how you see it, and how you interpret it for the people you serve, whoever your audience is.

"I do always start my stories with who I am," said Francis Hondal, former Mastercard executive advisor. She's a first-generation Cuban American, born and raised in Miami. She is incredibly proud of her heritage and how critical it's been to her success.

"This is so important to be true to yourself. To be able to express yourself, to be able to share your perspectives, which, in my case, being a Latina born and raised in a Hispanic community where we are the majority, not the minority, coming into a different environment for the most part in corporate America."

She told me she's been fortunate in her career to expand from being influenced by her Hispanic heritage and upbringing to becoming truly global. She credits her upbringing and her corporate career experience for stoking her interest in meeting different people and listening to different perspectives. However, she said that doesn't mean she doesn't have her own point of view. "I'm a pretty strong character that way. But I have really been conscious of how to collaborate and think differently by working in teams."

Perhaps more important, Francis recognizes it's perfectly fine that we don't have all the answers as individuals. Like many women in corporate America, she admits to getting impostor syndrome along the way when working alongside Ivy League–educated colleagues, those with different content knowledge than she had, and others who all seemed to have more value in the organization. She broke free from it when an advisor took her through a program that examined her strengths—along with the things she wasn't naturally good at. She learned that her facility with strategy and ability to connect people, teams, and groups that she absorbed at home from her parents' perspective and mindset as immigrant entrepreneurs was something unique she had that others didn't—and it couldn't really be taught. Armed with that knowledge, it became much easier for her to leave certain tasks to others and focus on what she did well.

Francis said that by getting really clear on her own value and where it came from, she became more mindful of how to best develop others' talents and what was needed to build strong teams for a thriving organization. "You can be a little bit more intentional about this is what I bring, and this is what's needed, then let's get this skill, get this experience, let's get this person in this situation. You've just got to raise that to your awareness and be okay with what you find out about yourself."

What you find out about yourself is what you use to distinguish yourself from others. Your number one differentiating factor is *you*: you have this unique set of qualities and experiences that have brought you to this place. But it can be difficult to realize where your value actually is because we often attach it to the bullet points on our résumé: the work experience that we have, the college degrees, the certifications and awards. This is especially true when we start new things, whether it's continuing our education, getting our first job, or starting a second career, hobby, or side hustle. Those are the times when we feel the least secure and the least connected to our value. To overcome that insecurity, start by asking these questions of yourself and of friends and family you trust who know you best: "What do I do that is special? What have others been surprised to learn about me or been impressed by that I thought was commonplace? What do I do that makes me, *me*? What do people seem to get from that?" Whether the answer is that you have a great sense of humor, are wonderful with children, can organize anything, or have an uncanny sense of direction, those are the things that could indicate what others might seek out, need from you—and pay you for.

I can't tell you how many times I've heard my students, when we talk about value, say in our first class, "But I've never had a job or real work experience, so I don't have any value to offer an employer beyond my education." Then I find out they coordinated food delivery services during the pandemic despite being stuck in their campus dorm rooms, or trained open water rescuers with the Red Cross, or volunteer taught at elementary schools in remote areas—not paid experiences but still valuable experiences.

Remember, all the things on your résumé mean something in theory, but they don't tell the whole story. That's where having the answers to these questions ready to round out those line items and make them come alive is really necessary. I mean, how many of us have worked with someone who had a great résumé but was really a horrible boss or a terrible coworker? Just like some people you've dated looked so good on paper and checked all the boxes, but the reality didn't live up to the window dressing? It's great to look qualified, but there's no point to it if there's no real value with it.

For me, offering our value is how we fulfill the transactional nature of being human. Value drives the constant flow of giving and receiving between and among people, connecting us to one another and ultimately creating community: What I do over here benefits others over there. Let's be clear—I do not mean this in the sense of quid pro quo, where you only do something in order to get something in return. That's an entirely different kind of exchange of value that I personally think we get drawn into far too much, reducing us to a constant game of one-upmanship, where keeping score and staying ahead is the goal, instead of fulfillment and satisfaction.

I consider this transference of value as being in service to one another: realizing that everything we do, and the way we do it in particular, affects others. Often what makes something worth doing is how useful or beneficial it is to someone else. Sometimes this happens intentionally, other times by happenstance. Think about artists who are moved to paint a landscape. They create their work from an internal desire, inspired by the beauty of what they see, using their talents to bring their vision to life. They may have created the artwork only for their own satisfaction, but there is still value for others who see and are moved by what they created. Then consider musicians who have a song in their heart that they want others to hear. They compose the song to perform it for others, and their satisfaction in creating the composition comes from seeing people enjoy, dance to, or be moved by their music. Both actions and their resulting creations add value to others, as well as to the creators, regardless of why they did it.

There are also things we do that are valuable, but we don't always know what that is—on purpose. We're not often told in what ways we uniquely provide value to others—sometimes because it's taken for granted, other times because it's not fully noticed, or worse, because it benefits someone else for us to stay unaware of what we're truly worth. There have been several times in my career when I compared notes with colleagues and found out how vastly underpaid I was for jobs I'd done well, mainly because I let the people I was working for convince me that I wasn't special and I was easily replaceable. That downplaying of value is a tactic managers and companies use to retain workers and get the most out of them for the least amount of money. That's just another reason for you to understand for yourself what you offer. Otherwise, we can get caught up in the functions of the job and checking those boxes, not realizing the value we bring in *how* we do them. When I was in radio full-time and any big music news broke, my producer Lisa E. would challenge herself to get that guest on the air with me within a certain number of calls (this was back before email—crazy, right?!). All producers know how to book a guest, but Lisa made it fun—and quicker! I missed it when we moved on to other shows, and I always compared other producers' last-minute booking abilities to hers. So, if you didn't do your job the way you do it, what would happen? How would your contribution be missed? Your answers will become clear as you work your way through this chapter.

Let's get to the core of your *Fearless Authenticity* by answering these three questions:

1. What work do you do and what is unique about how you do it?
2. What are the benefits others get from your work and the way you do it?
3. What is important to you about providing those benefits to others?

This process takes you on a journey where you can connect the things that you do with who you are and the way you move in the world. It will help you develop a succinct and clear way of stating your value so that others can easily understand who you are, what you do, and how you do it. It will also connect you and your work to the impact it has on other people. Having a way of talking about yourself and your work can help you get more opportunities by showing others where you and your skills fit, better results from networking and career communications, and subsequently more opportunities to move forward more easily toward your goals. This is true not only in how others receive this information, but in how you talk about yourself to yourself and reinforce what you're capable of in your own mind.

I tend to focus on work because we spend most of our lives working. It's easy to track value through it, but you can change that first question to focus on something else, because your value isn't just in your job. It's in who you are. So, maybe the question shifts to "What qualities or gifts do you have?" If you're not currently working, think about what work you want to do. Or if you're transitioning between careers, consider what you want to accomplish next and the actions that go along with that.

BACK TO MY FIRST QUESTION:

What work do you do
and what is unique about how you do it?

This definition of what you do and how you do it gives us a foundation upon which to build the story of your value. I'll give you a hint—it's not your job title or description. I often end up telling people what it's not, because they make

38

it more complicated than it has to be. We confuse our job descriptions with the work we actually do, the physical or mental tasks that it takes to achieve the objectives that are part of our job description. You are skilled—what does that actually mean you do every day? Maybe you manage the sales of your organization or your team. You could be a therapist, or a coach, or a disciplinarian for your employees, probably all three. Your functions and responsibilities could include conducting one-on-one meetings with your sales team or motivating your team in a sales meeting or analyzing your team's performance. If you tell me, "My job is to generate sales and revenue"—that's not your work. That's an explanation of the results your work delivers.

My clients or students will ask if this is just about tasks they do daily, or the outcomes of those tasks. Sometimes, it's both. Our daily tasks are usually repetitive, and that's the way we generate consistent results. Here, I want you to list those tasks in terms of significance—which actions do you take each day that are essential to reaching your job's goal? There's probably at least one that directly impacts your company's customers, even when you're not in a customer-facing role. Also note the way you do them that affects those results. Is the way you perform your work efficient? Does it produce quicker responses or make someone else's job on your team easier?

For instance, when I did a workshop for employees at a social services agency, a good number of employees there did not work directly with the clients who benefited from their services, even though their job titles, descriptions, and outcomes were tied to delivery of those services. Once they moved past their titles and focused on what they did every day, the answer to this question became clear. One man, we'll call him Steven, had a title that was something along the lines of client healthcare liaison, but he said instead of clients, he mostly talked to providers all day to resolve issues with claims. Steven shared that he had a knack for cutting through bureaucratic red tape with Medicaid and other insurers, in part because he had learned how to precisely code claims to reduce rejections and had developed relationships with adjusters that streamlined the process when resubmissions were required. His work on the providers' behalf enabled them to focus less on paperwork and more on delivering healthcare services to the organization's clients, one of his job outcomes. Steven was indeed a client healthcare liaison, but his daily tasks were more nuanced than his title suggested, and the way he approached his work with an eye for detail and building external relationships to assist with internal challenges was beneficial not only to the client, but for the provider in the middle. And that brings us to the . . .

SECOND QUESTION:

What are the benefits people get from your work and the way you do it?

As with Steven's story, this is where outcomes really come into play—connecting the benefits we provide to all the different stakeholders whom we touch with our work and the way we do it. Put simply, who's getting something out of what you do and the way you do it? This is the path to see where your worth is. Come up with three solid benefits that the work you do provides to other people. As you explore what those benefits are, certain words will pop up over and over again, leading to a theme that connects all your work.

I'll use my media work as an example here first. I started in radio because I loved music and loved to talk. As I went on, I realized that the talking part, especially interviewing people and telling stories, was what I did best and what I was being paid to do—creating content (even though we didn't call it that at the time) that listeners would come back day after day to hear. I got an opportunity later to host a television show and tried it out for fun. Once I got into it, it dawned on me that they had hired me to do the same things that I did on radio—interviewing people and sharing information—only without the music. My manager at the time told me that he loved my interviews because they were more like conversations, and I could get guests to share things no one had heard before, which made them compelling. He also told me the stories I shared and questions I asked listeners in calls on the air were real and relatable, so everybody could connect to them in some way. Then on the other side, listeners told me I was good company for them at work. It's one thing to produce content that serves as background noise for people throughout the day; it's another thing entirely to create shows and tell stories that give listeners a true feeling of connection and community—that was the benefit my style of work brought to others.

Now, I'll admit, I didn't follow the advice I'm giving now. It took other people telling me what I did to know how my work stood out. Once I knew that, I focused on developing those qualities further and using them everywhere I went. Much later, I noticed key words and phrases like *sharing, connecting,* and *telling stories* became themes that repeated throughout my work and gave me clues of all the other places my experience might also apply—which is how I started my business. (More on key words in a sec.) Just know that when you're aware of what your work means and what it provides to others, that opens the door to increasing its value.

When I spoke about knowing the value you bring to your work at a Dress for Success professional women's development program, an audience member told me afterward that she never thought much about how her work might benefit other people, even after her supervisor thanked her personally for her work. She was happy for the compliment, but as the assistant to the executives who ran the company, she still didn't think her job had much impact other than helping them. That is, until she thought about it during our session. She shared that her supervisor had expressed gratitude for how detail-oriented she was and the way she kept them all on track by catching errors and troubleshooting and reminding them about what she thought were rote, mundane tasks—like signing off on payroll. When she connected doing her job to something like making sure everyone was paid correctly on time, she realized the way she did her job was important to keeping the company functioning smoothly. Once she understood the contribution she made in that one area, it shifted her perspective on everything else. That's the power that knowing your value gives you.

Similar realizations of value are just as useful on the opposite end of the hierarchy. CurlMix CEO and cofounder Kim Lewis is a leader in naturally curly hair care. She said she's learned that one of the benefits of her work is giving her customers self-assurance through their hair.

"I've kind of come to realize that hair is almost how you see yourself sometimes," she said. "It can be the confidence that you need to walk into that job interview, or to ask for the pay that you deserve, or to advocate for yourself in the hospital. It can really empower you to become a better version of yourself. That really keeps me going and it reminds me of the purpose of what I do." And when Kim hears stories of how CurlMix changes her customers, she said, "That makes me feel like, okay, Kim, you made the right decision . . . this is what you're supposed to be doing."

EMPOWERMENT ENDORSEMENT

In the seven-plus years since I started my company, I would say 70 to 80 percent of the people I work with learn that empowering others is at least one of the benefits they provide. There's something very human about that. It may not be a primary directive, but I think that's where we find meaning in our work.

Is empowerment one of your desired benefits? If not, what is?

THIRD QUESTION:

What's important about
providing those benefits to others?

How do you feel about those benefits that your work provides to other people? Once you see it all written down, don't be shocked if suddenly you realize that you really give a shit about your job. Maybe not in a big picture, save-the-world kind of way . . . perhaps what you care about is the money and what it does for you and those you care about. A guy in one of my corporate training sessions told me that the main benefit of his job was a paycheck. He could provide for his family—his kids got to do their activities, they could take vacations, he could watch them play sports. He said he didn't feel one way or another about his job itself, but it made him happy to be able to take care of his wife and children.

Now, if you're a teacher, it may be more important to you to make sure your students are prepared for their next step. Or if you're a therapist, it may be helping people be at peace with their lives, able to love, forgive, move on, and not carry the steamer trunk of shit with them every day. So many different jobs, so many different benefits, depending on your priorities. It could be completely selfish—it doesn't matter. But why is it important to you? That's your purpose, that's why you get up every day. It's okay if it's petty or grandiose or simple. That awareness also gives you a clue to other things and other ways you can get that sense of importance for yourself. The same way retired athletes use their knowledge on the field to become coaches, you can transfer what you know and how you did it to a different role. An executive who loves developing and launching new products might use those skills to invest in and advise start-ups. Telling stories has always been important for me, so I asked myself how many different ways could I use that skill. I'm at about six and counting: radio, television, acting, speaking, teaching, and now writing. Keep asking yourself, *How can I amplify that? How can I scale that?*

When she started CurlMix, Kim Lewis knew she wanted to prioritize a commitment to her community. That meant creating great products for her community to utilize, but it also meant hiring people from the same neighborhood where the product is made.

"The way I get to impact my community is incredibly fulfilling. [For example,] When someone on my team tells me they bought their first house with their CurlMix paycheck or they bought an engagement ring for their boo or they're going back to school," she told me. "To know that we hire Black people from the South Side of Chicago, we manufacture right here at home. Plenty of people are like, 'Why don't you just manufacture overseas for cheap?' Because I want to impact the community where I live."

There are times when the biggest impact you want to make is even closer to home. What's important to us changes over time. Exploring that while understanding the full scope and applications for the value in our work and how we do it can guide us to pivot in a way that better serves our lives in that moment. One of my colleagues in Chicago television did that when her priorities shifted.

Anupy Singla made the tough decision to leave her job as a morning TV business reporter in Chicago when her two daughters were babies. She was compelled to make the career change because she worried about what they were eating while she was at work (she felt so bad, she often cried in the live truck while she was out reporting). She has such a strong connection to the food of her Indian heritage that she wanted to make sure they felt it, too.

"You're in the station at 3:00 a.m. It's just a lot. . . . I couldn't not cook the way I wanted to; the way my mother had for us," she shared with me. "So, it really for me was this moment of, okay, what do I want more? What's most important? How do I make this happen? And really it was just this idea to take a break. Let me cook all of the foods that I've grown up with and I love for my two girls who were babies back then."

She said her girls embraced the cuisine and have grown up to be amazing eaters.

"Your day-to-day is a food you love. I think, for me, the idea was to give them something I didn't have," she told me. "I was embarrassed of the food we had in the house because no one really knew back then . . . what Indian was."

Anupy took advantage of being at home and used her skills to write four cookbooks, sharing the family recipes that she learned cooking with her grandfather in India and giving her daughters a powerful legacy.

"They're really proud of not just books, not just me, but the food, and that was my goal. I'm so proud of that."

Anupy's career path could be a case study about answering my three questions. She had to reexamine the value she was putting out into the world and determine if it was still in alignment with her goals: What work am I doing now? What are the benefits? What's important to me about it? She realized that she wanted to be more present in her children's lives and share her culture not only with them, but with the rest of the world through cookbooks and a line of spices and sauces from her company, Indian as Apple Pie. To get there, she had to make adjustments and decide if her new plan matched the life she wanted to live. When she started those conversations with herself in the live truck, that led to other conversations of how to get it done.

When you have those conversations with yourself about your value and authenticity, remember that you already have every single thing you need inside you. That knowledge is the key that unlocks every single door you're trying to open, or maybe break down depending on your spirit. That's where you'll find your *Fearless Authenticity*. Our biggest successes are found in who we really are as these amazing stories have already shown. We all individually have something very particular that we are here to do on this earth, and the closer we get to expressing and living in our truest gifts and talent and the farther away we get from doing and living how we think others want us to, the more likely every single action we take and decision we make will lead to achieving whatever it is that we want most of all and are meant to do. They kind of come together quite easily.

BE YOU
AUTHENTICITY ACTION

To *Be You*, you must know yourself. It's time to get real about discovering and knowing your value. Answer these questions and, as I mentioned, you'll see a theme emerge.

- What work do you do or want to do and what is unique about how you do it?

- What are the benefits others get from your work and the way you do it?

- What's important to you about providing those benefits to others?

CHAPTER 3

Walk in Your Power

"If you don't know who you are, you won't act with the power you have."

Read that again: "If you don't know who you are, you won't act with the power you have."

Those potent words come from my colleague Brenda Darden Wilkerson, president and CEO of AnitaB.org. She is a fearless leader in technology and the epitome of authenticity. However, she, too, has struggled to answer the *Authenticity Action* questions from chapter 2:

- What work do you do and what is unique about how you do it?

- What are the benefits others get from your work and the way you do it?

- What's important to you about providing those benefits to others?

Brenda went to Northwestern University with the intention of becoming a doctor; it had been her dream since she was a little girl to help others. It was a dream her mother encouraged over her artsy aspirations. About halfway through her pre-med biochemical engineering program, she realized the obstacles were bigger than she anticipated—and unexpected. She was one of few women in the program and among a handful of Black people and was already feeling isolated in a way she'd never felt before.

Then, a professor in class bluntly asked her, "Why are you here?" She was discouraged, but not defeated. As she continued her coursework, she learned that medicine and the way it was practiced in this country weren't what she thought they were, and certainly not aligned with how she wanted to help people. So, she had a choice to make. By that point, Brenda had already taken a couple computer science classes as part of her major requirements that sparked her interest in technology, so she set aside medicine and pivoted to a different way to serve.

"You change when you allow yourself to see what gives you that spark when you're doing it," she said. "Some of us, because we've been trained, know how to do several things, so we just do what we're told." Brenda realized having that spark about something she was able to do meant it wasn't just a job—it was the thing she was supposed to be doing at that point in time. Knowing that set her free—and she also found technology fulfilled her childhood love of creativity:

50

"I've always wanted to create and I've always wanted to have an impact on a lot of people."

That, she has. Brenda created the Computer Science for All program that integrated tech learning into the core curriculum of Chicago Public Schools, becoming the model for computer science education across the country in 2016 when then president Barack Obama made it a national initiative.

But still, Brenda didn't fully perceive her value and impact. It wasn't until they took the initiative to New York and a colleague told her the program was rolled out to 1.1 million students that it finally started to dawn on her.

When I asked Brenda why she didn't recognize her power at first, her answer was a common one among many women I know and work with: "I'm definitely focused on the work of it. But I don't think that's unique to me. I think a lot of women, and may I say Black women, are just about doing the work. It's just about getting it done, having the impact, and knowing that, underneath there, we've got to do way, way, way, way more than others to prove ourselves."

THE WAY TO SUCCESS

Walking in power is something I'm still learning because what I value about what I do is mostly what I think other people value about me. But I'm finding there's a whole bunch of skills I have that people value that I haven't been trading on. I think a lot of us are like that, especially women.

We, as women, think that the way to success is getting stuff done, because for us, that *is* the way to success. You get the kids dressed and off to school, the dog walked, the to-do list at work accomplished, the family fed and put to bed—you've had a successful day. That's all stuff that nobody notices. Why? Because it got done.

In fact, the only time anybody takes notice is when it doesn't get done. Then we get blamed for not doing it. Remember that time on social media when women posted videos of what happened when they stopped picking up after their family members and left everything sitting right where they left it? It got some pretty passionate responses for work that most deem invisible.

Many of us choose not to talk about all the work we do at home or on our jobs, because we don't want to seem like we're complaining or comparing our workloads to others. But all our work deserves to be acknowledged. We need to talk about it. We must tell our story. That's the only way it will ever count.

So, be your own best advocate and publicist. You don't have to share every detail, especially at work; the highlights will do. Tell your story in three quick and easy steps:

1. This is what I did today.

2. This is what happened.

3. This is how we got here.

You don't have to tell a narrative every time. But you've got to tell something.

Despite Brenda's phenomenal success with Computer Science for All, that work mindset carried over to attaining her position at AnitaB.org. While Brenda inspired audiences with her message that they can do anything, she found herself doubting her own abilities when she was approached for her role at AnitaB.org.

"I didn't even call the recruiter for two months," she said, recounting how she fought against the opportunity. "When I finally called him, I argued with him for another two weeks. Why would they want me? I didn't understand."

Brenda had to learn for herself her own value, even while she was preaching that to everybody else—not just for herself, but so she could do the work she was called to do. You have to know what you offer somebody and what it means to you to be able to do whatever it is you want.

You do that by turning my core questions from chapter 2 into a value proposition or mission statement for yourself. The basic value proposition template I use is: *I help X with Y to do Z.* You can substitute words like "serve," "collaborate," or "work with" for *help*, or "get" or "accomplish" for *do,* depending on how you want to express the way you work and interact with others.

My questions are out of order, but the answers are all there:

> X = the people who benefit from your work
>
> Y = the work that you do and how you do it
>
> Z = can be a mix of the work that you do, how you do it, and why you do the work (in terms of the benefits or what it means to you)

Here's how that template fits my work: I am a speaker, consultant, television and radio personality with thirty years of broadcast experience (Y) who helps individuals and organizations (X) find more success and deliver their unique authentic value (Z) through visionary leadership and inspired speaking.

Authentic value and success are what I value as benefits to others. I want people to be happy; I want people to get what they want, preferably as easily as possible. Visionary leadership and inspired speaking lead to that outcome.

So, when you take the answers to those questions and turn them into this declarative statement, you have an affirmation of your value that backs you up every time you walk into a room or share your opinions on-screen. As useful as that statement is in explaining to others what you do and the value you bring, you never actually have to say it out loud to anyone to be able to walk in your power. Just the knowledge of the impact you have had and intend to have helps you do that. You've got to know what you're bringing to the table for you to sit down at it, or even flip it over, if you need to. You communicate to other people what you believe about yourself, no matter the situation, so, you've got to own it.

Christin Zollicoffer is chief diversity, equity, and inclusion (DEI) officer for a major healthcare system in the Northeast. She was new to the C-suite when she reached out for some coaching on how to raise her leadership game. She didn't feel like she was operating at the same level as her peers despite previous leadership positions.

During one of our early sessions, she told me: "Everyone else has tons of letters behind their name. And when I say tons, I mean tons . . . I don't have a master's degree. I have my PMP [project management professional] certification, but that's all that it is. So, what is my value?"

It wasn't just the credentials intimidating Christin. Her vision of herself as a leader included shortcomings in other categories, such as the way she crafted messages, the way she framed questions, and how she used her voice, including the way she sounded out loud and her style of speaking. To help her create her value proposition and hone in on the unique qualities she offered, I adapted my core questions to be more applicable to her situation. Not just what work she does, but how does she see the leadership that others do and that she is aspiring to? What does she perceive in them?

She shared with me five leadership qualities she wished she had: the ability to delegate and let go of details; quantifiable knowledge at her disposal; the ability to network; the ability to operate at a level of high quality; and a degree of smoothness, grace, and composure.

"What about those do or do not resonate with who you are right now or the value you bring to a situation?" I asked.

"All of those. I feel as though I expect a level of quality but it's not like top tier . . . I feel like there's a gap there. The reason I hold those qualities in admiration is because I don't see them in myself."

After further discussion, Christin acknowledged she had some of those qualities, but not enough to feel confident in them. She conceded that she could let go of details up to a point and was adept at networking—it just didn't always resonate with her. I explained to her that in talking through how she sees leaders and understands her value exchange (how she delivers her unique value to others), we could marry those ideas with what she is, who she is, and her personal values to develop a leadership value proposition that acts as her power base.

To get there, we dug deeper into her perceptions of leadership qualities and their true utility and necessity.

"Are those qualities the key to those people's ability to lead?" I asked. "Are they essential to their success as leaders?"

She quickly answered that they're not essential. That response led me to my next set of questions: If you have five elements in each hand—five qualities you admire in other people's leadership styles in one hand, and five ways that you see or don't see yourself in the five qualities in the other hand—what can you let go of or reshape in a way that's more authentic to you? Since she admired five key leadership qualities:

- the ability to delegate and let go of the details,

- quantifiable knowledge at their disposal,

- the ability to network,

- the ability to operate at a level of high quality,

- and a degree of smoothness, grace, and composure

and acknowledged that she was pretty good at two of them, I wanted to see if she could change how she saw the other three qualities on her list and still define her own authentic leadership style as valid without them. Even though she admired those qualities, there was something bigger lingering in her self-image as a leader that I wanted to get at.

"If these things are not essential to success and they're not vital to what you want to do," I said, "then why do you want to incorporate them into your leadership style?"

To Christin, it was all about gaining ground. "It's an ideal," she said. "As a competitor, you always think about closing the gap. It doesn't mean it's required, doesn't mean you're not successful in the moment, but you think about closing the gap." She then had an aha moment, picking up on what I was hoping she would.

She asked me, "Can you just appreciate where you are?"

Bingo! That's where I wanted her to land. She had been striving so hard to see herself as proficient in the same categories as the leaders she admired by incorporating the things she thought she lacked, when in fact she had something better.

We took it a step further and made a list of the leadership qualities she already had to counterbalance the qualities in others that didn't work for her and how she delivered her value. However, what we really needed to do was not just close the gap on what those qualities were, but determine the abilities she was far stronger in; defining her leadership in a way that was equivalent to, if not matching, theirs.

"The reality is you are in this league now with those same people," I said, "and you didn't get there by mistake. You know that."

Where Christin excels is in relational leadership, a style that emphasizes empathy and empowerment in building team skills and fostering better relationships as a foundation for progress.

"I don't call it work," she told me. "It's what I do in my spare time, that's all the time, that's who I am . . . I didn't realize until just now that I'm helping people who report to me or whom I can bring something to." With that revelation, she strengthened her purpose.

"That is your value proposition for all people [in the organization]," I said. "I would even argue, not just the people under you on the organization chart, but the people adjacent to you, and perhaps above you as well. I think it's about stretching your perception of the value you bring."

It really wasn't that big a stretch to look at the leadership abilities she aspired to and see how the ones she already had were really just the other sides of the same coins. For example, remember she talked about being good at networking? Makes sense, because networking at its core, even though it's often carried out at a surface level, is truly about building relationships over time and that was her number one quality—she knew she owned it from the way she consistently developed and maintained relationships in a very purposeful way. Her challenge was in making the correlation between the two and recognizing her value.

That's the trick to seeing and believing in your value. So often we try to close what we see as gaps in our abilities or qualities, when there isn't really a gap to fill. We get pulled into that trap when we compare ourselves to others and focus on qualities they have, only seeing them as more valuable than ours because we don't have them. That's an illusion, just another faulty belief. And if you believe you fall short in some way in comparison to others, you will have a tell—a part of you that will betray your perceived shortcoming. That part of you will speak differently to those in power than those who are not. It will apologize for not being what you think you should be. Whatever you

WALK IN YOUR POWER

believe, you will behave accordingly. And not walk in the power you do have.

To help Christin close the gaps she saw in herself earlier for good, free from any doubts, I gave her a homework assignment to focus on using her strongest qualities that she identified and see how they worked in action on a similar dimension to the ones she felt deficient in before. During this time, she was adding to her team, presenting frequently, building and managing more partner relationships, and working on a long-term strategy to implement the changes needed to achieve the organization's diversity, equity, and inclusion (DEI) goals she'd been hired to accomplish. She had ample opportunities to walk in her power as a visionary and relational leader who invites her team to become better versions of themselves through communication, collaboration, and co-creation with compassion and empathy.

The most beautiful thing was that those were all the qualities she had listed as her most valuable when we started working together, with a few additions as she made discoveries along the way. She always saw that value as serving her work and what she was hired to do, but contrary to what she feared, those strengths also sustained her at this new level in the functions she needed to fulfill. I think it was more evident through the way she did her work than in anything she actually said to others. Her team was secure, she was moving forward with ease, and she no longer felt lacking because she wasn't trying to adopt qualities that didn't fit her strengths.

What we believe about ourselves, our work, and how we do it are key parts of our success. We communicate those beliefs to others, often before we enter a room or utter a word. Those beliefs affect what we say and how we say it. If you don't have conviction in those beliefs, how will anybody else?

One of my media colleagues worked in TV news for thirty years, writing and producing all kinds of content. When she left the business, she did freelance work that still involved creating content on new platforms. But she wrangled with what to call herself. It took several years and some serious self-reflection for her to be comfortable calling herself a writer.

I shook my head at her on many occasions, failing to understand her hesitation. But in her head, she clung to the idea that a writer was a professional who wrote best-selling novels or published serious stories; she didn't consider her newswriting for TV worthy of the writer title. Now, she uses the affirmation "I am a writer" to reinforce her accomplishments, reach her goals, and walk in her power. Her value proposition could be: I am an experienced writer (Y) who helps individuals, businesses, and organizations (X) tell their stories to better engage their audiences and grow their success (Z) through dynamic content and strategic execution.

That is the strength you gain from knowing who you are and what you do. How you talk about yourself is important, including affirmations and acknowledgments. The reality is that when we talk about what we're *not*, we shut down pathways. Nobody can create something out of a negative. This is a simplified example, but if somebody asked me, "Hey, you're in television, you must know how to edit video, right?" and I reply, "No, I'm not an editor," that answers the question, but it closes the door and cuts off any further exchange or creation. Look for the other things that you are: "I may not be able to edit video, but I'm great at being a host and presenting on-camera, and I know some great editors, too." Then I've opened the door to keep the exchange going.

That's how words have power. They turn on or shut off circuits in our brain, enabling us to move forward or preventing us from seeing how the things we do are good for ourselves and others. If we can't tap into that, how are we going to convince anybody else to? To me, that's the connection to success. That's the connection to power. Being able to say unequivocally with no shame when walking into a room, "This is what I do well—you're going to miss out," even if you don't say it like that. To walk into an interview or a work situation and be like, "This is something I can do, I can work with."

That's how my career in television got going. I had been doing guest spots on a couple local shows, standing where people told me to stand, saying what they told me to say, adding my little razzle-dazzle to it. But I never did any of my own producing or reporting. A producer for an arts and entertainment show had seen me, liked what I did on the other shows, and reached out because she had a position for a reporter covering the local arts scene. I was excited and ready to go, until she told me I had to produce my own packages (what we call *segments*). I was heartbroken, but I told her up front that as much as I loved TV and wanted to be a reporter, I'd never done it before except on radio.

Her response took me by surprise: "Girl, stop, you're already doing the hard part on-camera that nobody can really teach you. That part you don't know is easy. I can explain how to do it in a few hours, and you'll either get it or you won't. And if you don't, the job's not for you."

I did figure it out, so I guess it was for me. I'll be honest, though, I don't know how much our system actually supports that kind of discovery anymore. We're always trying to qualify and justify; you have to get a certification for this and need a degree for that. I'm not against any of that, exactly the opposite—I have a couple degrees myself and each one has served me well. But it seems to me that many people think they need them for the wrong reasons and end up disappointed when they don't get what they were expecting.

If you're trying to deepen your knowledge in a formal way, or if the expertise you seek is only available that way, it makes sense. Your education is always worth it because no one can take it away from you. But if you're looking for permission, validation, or approval to do something new, the question becomes whether the degrees and certifications and ROIs (returns on investment) are really what you need. When you are living in your fearless authenticity, you are connected to a deeper knowing of yourself and your abilities. It is a knowing that is led by your limitless potential, not by your endorsed skills on LinkedIn. Just like *Fearless Authenticity* is for you and not others, your degrees and certifications are for you and your expansion, even if you use them to sell yourself to others in order to get what you want, need, and desire. Getting degrees and certifications will feel fulfilling if they help you get closer to who you are, knowing what you offer, and making that connection inside yourself *for yourself.* But pursuing it for external validation will not give the deep knowing that you deserve what you're working for; only your belief in yourself can do that. Whatever your struggle is in seeing your value (and you are not alone in that), having a degree or certification for its own sake will never convince you or anybody else. If I've said it once, I've said it a million times: validation comes from within when you have no doubt about who you are and what your value is.

Dr. Ian Smith, a physician, fitness expert, TV personality, and author, is the perfect example of someone who knew his purpose from the very beginning and never wavered. He told me he never planned to go against the traditional stereotype of a doctor in a suit and white coat.

"It wasn't me making a conscious decision that I'm not going to be this buttoned-up guy. My conscious decision was that I want to be who I am . . . I wasn't a typical medical student. . . . I was a guy who loved music and going out. I loved sports, lifting weights, I love all kinds of things. Meanwhile, a lot of medical students were in the library eight hours a day after school . . . I was just as serious as everyone else, but I didn't believe I had to be a certain way to express my seriousness to become a good doctor."

And he knew from the jump that people wouldn't always understand what he was bringing to the table, like when he started doing TV. People would say to him, "You spent all that time to become a doctor, and now you're on TV?" But when his broadcasts started doing well, everyone changed their tune. They started telling him how great he was and how awesome his work was.

"My whole thing is, I'm already there," Dr. Ian said. "I'm waiting for you, you'll eventually get there. But I'm already there. I've never let it bother me."

Dr. Ian said it's easy for people to judge you and have expectations of who you are and what you're worth, but you can't let that cloud your perspective.

"I'll never forget one day I'm on the subway, on the train heading downtown, and a lady says to me, 'Dr. Ian?' I was like, 'Yeah.' She was like, 'You ride the subways?' I'm like, 'Yeah, I'm a New Yorker. How do you expect me to get around?' . . . The point is how people see you and what they expect of you sometimes is very different than how you see yourself and what you expect of yourself. You always have to be true to who you are."

Being true to yourself. Sounds simple. But don't be confused—simple is not easy. It is hard work. It is commitment. It's love to and for yourself, as Dr. Ian so confidently illustrates. Walking in your power is knowing what is valuable about you; what you know about how you interpret things, and offering it. Because you're saying: "This is who I am. This is what I know. This is how I'm different from other people." And knowing what you believe about yourself gives you the confidence to reveal your true self to others.

BE YOU
AUTHENTICITY ACTION

What do you know about your true self?

Write down your beliefs about yourself—what is true and not true?

PART II

FOUNDATIONS FOR SUCCESS

LIVE IT, TELL IT, SELL IT

CHAPTER 4

Live It

We've been communicating since the moment we came out of the womb: that first cry each of us had as babies was the first story we told, announcing we had arrived in the world. But because we've been doing it since birth, we take it for granted and we often don't work on it. And that lack of intention leads to missed connections. Making the connection that comes through people's real stories is what's important to me. It's what I've tried to do my whole life. The way we talk about what's important to us is the way we get to *Fearless Authenticity*.

When you talk about yourself to your audience, whether it's through an Instagram story, a work presentation, or your podcast, you have to ask yourself: What's the whole point? Connection, no doubt about it. And let me tell you something right now: connection is essential because that's what we're all seeking wherever we are—social media, in person, with clients, on a Zoom call. Connection gives us friendship, strong work relationships/network, love, closed sales. People follow those they feel connected to and vice versa.

My three foundations of successful communication are: *Live It, Tell It, Sell It. Live It* is about you. *Tell It* is about what you're talking about. *Sell It* is about the people you're talking to. Together, they are a formula that applies to everything we do—working, speaking, leading, selling, living—because we have to find connection to accomplish most anything, and understanding/executing all the components of good communication is the way that happens.

Let's dig into foundation number one.

Live It is understanding who we are and being aware of how that impacts other people. Building a connection starts with you: what you say, how you say it, and considering others is important . . . and it's only possible when you take responsibility for your part first. That was brought home to me clearly when I was sharing my dating woes with my friend's dad. After listening to my whole story, his only reaction was to ask, "Jeanne, you ever stop to think maybe it's you?" And it was me. Maybe not all me, but it started with me. We create connections and experiences together. We must start with us.

When taken to the extreme, this awareness could look like changing or hiding something about yourself to be what others need you to be. That's not what we're talking about. We're talking about understanding your range and understanding how to use it in a conscious way: to say what it is you need to say, do what it is you need to do, and accomplish your purpose in being there. Part of that understanding is realizing you may be doing things subconsciously that counteract your goals.

You can never, ever, control how people perceive you, but you can control what *you* do. Ask yourself: Is what I intended to communicate what is being perceived? So many things can get in the way of our message—the biggest one is us. Whatever we're feeling or thinking—whether we're nervous or confident—comes through what we say. Even if we think we're hiding it well, we're communicating that to people in all sorts of ways. I think a lot of us walk around thinking we're doing one thing, when in reality, people see us in a whole other way.

You can control everything you do/say/present . . . but not what people do with it. You have to be able to let that go. Some people are bound and determined to take stuff the way that they want to take it and sometimes you gotta let them. The thing is, if you're not aware, and you just wing it, then you're not doing your part in whatever conversation or exchange you're having. Part of this awareness is understanding how you impact people. Most of us understand this on some level, usually unconsciously. When it's elevated to a conscious effort, that's when it's useful as a tool to understand how to have the effect you want to have on others.

As much as I love words and as many I have said in my lifetime so far, I know that words are not the only key to connecting . . . the way you say the words is as important as the words themselves, if not more.

Before the human brain developed true speech, we were still able to communicate without words. Our "lizard brain" (see the sidebar on the following page) still processes our emotions in a similar way—we sense the meaning before we fully hear and process the words. For instance, what happens when we hear someone's tone of voice? The person could be giving you a compliment, but it doesn't sound like it. Some people call that a backhanded compliment. My grandmommy called it "nice nasty." And she could really dish it out. You'd hear the words but immediately know you'd messed all the way up.

WHAT DO I MEAN BY LIZARD BRAIN?

"Lizard brain" usually refers to the limbic system of the brain, which controls all of our instinctual survival actions and reactions like fight, flight, feeding, fear, and freezing up. It's called "lizard brain" because the limbic system is about all a lizard can count on for brain function.

Live It focuses on how all those nonverbal elements play together. To become more aware of what you're doing, pay attention to your body language—facial expressions, gestures, eye contact, body position and posture; the tone, volume, and the way you use your voice; what you do when you listen to and respond to questions. All of that goes into the impact you have on others—without ever really saying a word.

The biggest problem people have is that they think they know how they come across to others, but they don't. So, they blame others—that they misunderstood—when it's really a combo of how each person participated in creating that moment. But if just one person in the exchange takes responsibility for how they come across and adjusts for what they intend, it can shift the whole thing.

My foolproof method of **Record**, **Review**, **Refine** will improve your awareness. If you have something important to say, try it out on yourself first. Record yourself saying it. Then, like a quarterback on Monday morning, review the tape so you can see yourself the way others see you.

If you understand what you do and how others experience you, you will know for sure if they understood you as you intended. You want to answer two questions:

1.   Is what I intended to say what was received?
2.   Did anything in our nonverbal communication distract or detract from that message?

You need to know what you're communicating to people, if what you're creating is coming across as planned, if your inner thoughts can be seen on your face or in your body language. Some poker players wear a hoodie and sunglasses in an effort to disguise any changes in their behavior—or "tells," as they're called—giving away their hand, good or bad. The same could be said for you—if you don't know how others perceive you, you don't know what your "tells" even are. You also have to be aware of any verbal tics or filler words you use when speaking. Verbal tics may be using "um" or "ah" repeatedly, distracting the audience from what you're saying. Same goes for filler words, such as "you know" or "like" to fill in gaps when you're thinking about what comes next in your presentation.

Consistency is the key to aligning your intention with others' perceptions. That's more likely when all your modes of communication match your words: verbal, nonverbal, emotional content, tone, body language, gestures, expressions, and so on. The best way to achieve that is practice! Let's say you have a job interview. You can pretty much predict the questions they'll ask. Record yourself answering them and then review it: Is what you intended to communicate taken as a whole? Is everything consistent? Is your nonverbal behavior backing up your words? If you say you're confident, do you look confident? Do you believe the whole package? Are you doing something distracting while you're speaking? Distractions take people out of your messaging and they shut down on you. I know someone who didn't get a job because she tapped her fingernails on the table, grating on the interviewer's nerves and distracting others to the point where they couldn't hear what she was saying. When it happened, my colleague said, "If she does that in every meeting she's in, I will never hear a word she's saying."

That's the whole point of *Live It*: Look at yourself and take it all in. Experience yourself the way other people do. It's about understanding who you are, how that affects other people, and how you can shift things and be better understood within your authentic range of expression. How are you going to best tailor that to the people with whom you talk? It's easy to increase your chances of success by just being aware of and making small shifts in how you express yourself that's closer to the truth of who you are and what you want to say.

That's the reason I have clients and students do the **Record**, **Review**, **Refine** exercise and why they fight me so hard about it. Once you realize how you affect other people, it then becomes your responsibility to change. At first, nobody wants to do it (they don't want to see themselves on camera), but they always come around.

You may think, *How is that possible?* So many of us are on camera every day, thanks to smartphones. There's a big difference between the relationship we have with the cameras on our phones and a separate video camera. The camera on our phone can be used for the purpose of improvement; we just tend not to. People see it differently because our phones live in our purses and pockets every day. We've become accustomed to how we see ourselves in that camera. It's not just a comfort with the camera, it's a comfort with what we see in it. It's the way we record ourselves, and the types of things we usually record with our phones won't show us what we're really doing. When you shoot yourself in a real-life situation or a mock-up of one, you're not doing a selfie or goofing off in a dance; you're seeing yourself "in the wild," your natural habitat. It's also the reason people get caught on camera—nobody notices phones anymore. When I show up with a video camera, the temperature immediately changes in the room. One or two show-offs might be willing to be taped, but that scenario is rare.

I can relate because I wasn't an eager participant when my mama started this kind of work with me. As a musician and vocal coach, she knew early on what I was capable of when she heard and watched me speak. Every time I recited a poem in church or performed a skit at school or gave a book report or speech, Mama coached me on my performance. She had me practice in front of her as if I were onstage, recorded it on an old-school cassette recorder—no video—and made me review the audiotape, which I hated. I didn't like hearing my voice. She would then ask me, "Is that how you wanted it to sound when you said it?" That's where the process started. Of course, later I realized she was giving me a way to do well, always improve at the things I cared about, and understand how my audience would receive what I was doing. I have to admit that for the longest time I thought she was trying to teach me how to be perfect but the main things she taught me were how to get better every time I did something, no matter how good I already thought I was; how to develop my best work and become my most authentic self in a way that truly connected with my audience.

My mama's (and now my) process is a must-do to perform well and improve your content delivery, because it really is about how well you're able to convey your ideas in the way you intend. What you say and your internal experience saying it are often very different from how it's perceived when others hear it. We're frequently unaware of how we impact people until we watch ourselves in a recording. After watching themselves, almost every one of my clients and students have said some version of, "Oh, wow, I had no idea I was doing that!" or "I can't believe it came out that way . . . that's not what I meant at all!" Anybody can tell you how they understood what you said, but until you see for yourself what that looks and feels like, it remains their perception, maybe even "their problem." Once you witness any mismatch between what you intended to say and how it came across, you have the power to align those two things. It might be as simple as using a different tone or gesture or becoming more aware of how you use your personal space. You've just got to see it first.

As you make adjustments to your delivery, pay close attention to how you're feeling about the changes you make—be sure they honor your authentic self and style. We all have a range of expression that's still true to who we are, while adaptive to what's appropriate in a variety of situations. Straying beyond that will rob others of the gift of who you are and what you're here to do. The more of us who express our truest selves in ways that others can hear and understand us, the more people will feel free to do the same and the better off we'll all be.

Something I've found to be true from my lifetime of working in radio and television is how everything fits together when you're communicating clearly on all levels. The smallest gesture can make a big difference—that's where your power comes from. When you know how you affect people, you can impact them in the way you need to and in the way they need you to. While your audience's perception of you will, of course, still be their own, your one job is to make sure they understood your intention, that what you are communicating—your message—is unmistakable. There's no confusing industry jargon, your body language exudes confidence, your tone relays your belief in what you're saying—you own it!

Remember your audience is whomever you're talking with, which includes your clients, your boss, your colleagues, your spouse, or your children. Even what you don't say is communicated in not-so-subtle ways. I saw this play out in such a powerful way in one of my leadership trainings. Two women in the group, Linda and Vanessa, volunteered to be recorded so everyone could experience **Record**, **Review**, **Refine** and see their interactions on-screen. Linda bravely shared an experience with a colleague with whom she had difficult conversations; she didn't feel heard and felt like something was missing from their interactions. I had her re-create a conversation with Vanessa, and when she challenged Linda about an aspect of a project, I could see in Linda's face she had something to say to counter her attack but instead she swallowed—audibly. She was literally swallowing her words.

When we reviewed the footage, I paused at that moment and asked Linda, "If you were sitting on the other side, how would you perceive that action?

She sat back and said: "It looks resistant. It feels like I'm not saying what I'm thinking, and I'm actually not."

"Do you really think your silence isn't telling somebody something?" I asked.

She admitted she felt silenced by this person. She started crying, realizing that she was still communicating the thoughts and emotions she believed she was controlling.

Now that she knew she did this and what it looked like to her colleague, we worked on how to modify the exchanges with this colleague, anticipating the difficult places and taking a moment to center and then respond. We also worked on understanding what her intention was with these conversations and what she wanted to create with her colleague instead. She realized she was going into these meetings afraid something bad was going to happen, so every choice she made reflected that fear.

Preparing herself included getting clear with how she felt about it, and what she wanted from it, her expectations. If she anticipated it was going to be a difficult conversation, she wanted it to be the least difficult it could be. She wanted it to end in agreement or at least peace. If she was itching for a fight, to get all her feelings out in the open, it wouldn't be pleasant, but it may have been what best served the moment.

She just had to be intentional and authentic about what she wanted to communicate.

That emotional aspect is what trips up a lot of folks, especially in work situations. Most of us avoid or try to hide our emotions because we want to stay in control and not be seen as "emotional." Ironically, hiding emotions will almost certainly give them away. It's the tell of all tells.

See, you may have the most cogent argument or logical explanation prepared, but your emotions will still leak out. Here's the thing most people don't fully understand and resist accepting: *Whatever you believe is what you're going to communicate.* If you're standing in front of an audience and believe you have something of value to share, everything you say and do will be infused with and support that belief . . . and your audience will feel and sense it, too, making it much more likely that they will listen, pay attention, and believe what you do.

Conversely, if you're nervous or afraid and you don't deal with or counter those emotions in some way, you will communicate that feeling to your audience. And nobody likes fear—it's an automatic turn-off and they tune out, even if they don't know exactly where it's coming from. Ever see a comedian bomb onstage? It's really hard to watch . . . almost as hard as it is for that pour soul onstage just trying to get some laughs. Try as they might, unless they can change the feeling they're giving the audience, it's over for that night.

Comedy legend George Wallace had his share of bombs early in his career. "I had to do forty-five minutes," he remembers. "I went onstage. Minute one, I got nothing. Minute two, I've got nothing. Kept going up to minute forty-five, nothing. . . . I'm dying up here. I'm talking, it hurt—your throat, your body, your head, your mind; you're in bad shape." George's advice for overcoming that failure is to get right back up onstage the next night. That's what he did, and he continued to make people laugh for the next five decades. Now, you may never be in a situation as difficult, but remember that when it's uncomfortable, people stop listening.

One way to shift an emotion that's off-putting to your audience is to first acknowledge you have it. So many people deny they're nervous or afraid and do a good job of convincing themselves of that lie until they hit the stage or podium. Then they're a wreck up there with no exit plan. As the saying goes, the first step to solving a problem is admitting that there is one. There are lots of ways to find calm in a sea of chaos, but if you can't get there in the moment, you can still shift how your audience experiences you. The trick is connecting the feeling you're sharing with your audience to a similar but more positive state of being. For example, the physical experience of being nervous is similar to excitement, so one way to start the shift is: "I'm so excited to be here to share something, I hope you'll be excited about, too! Please forgive me if I seem a little nervous—I just need to calm down so I can get it all out." That's something that anybody can understand, and you've given them someplace good to go with what they're getting from you. Really, who doesn't want to be excited sometimes? It might work, it might not, but if you don't ask for a little grace from your audience, you won't get it and all you'll have is an audience, whether it's two people or two hundred, who know for sure something is wrong.

Your **Record**, **Review**, **Refine** sessions may not be as revealing (or emotional) as Linda's, but it's an opportunity to think and get intentional about what you're doing, and it's also an opportunity for feedback.

Giving yourself feedback, however, is not easy. It's an art. You want to balance seeing the successful things you already do with being honest about the things that need improvement. Be kind because anything less will kill the confidence you should have in getting this far. Remember that it's easier to build on the good things that you already have than it is to increase your capacity for the things you don't have yet. First, look for at least three things you did well before you look for anything to improve. If you're still having trouble after that, pretend you're watching someone else. If you're beating yourself up over your performance, give feedback to someone else with whom you can be kind but honest, then do the same for yourself.

Now, despite all your efforts to communicate clearly, there's always the chance that a person you're talking to is a jerk or your audience is unforgiving or maybe even hostile and it won't matter what you do or say. Just realize that if you already believe that about them, you're going to treat them as such. Just be honest about what you're doing and understand how you participate in it. It's easy to place blame on other people and ignore how we participate in the exchange. Every time we have an exchange with somebody, we are cocreating our experience together. Very rarely is it one-sided, and if it is, you will feel that energy drain because people will let it happen. If somebody isn't receiving what you're saying, yes, you have to consider their part in it. But also consider yours. I suggest looking at how you contributed to it because that's the only thing you can control and change.

After my friend's father told me "maybe it's you" in my dating debacles, I immediately knew he was right and that I couldn't blame everything on the guys I was dating. It was time for me to do something about it. Turns out, one of my biggest issues was I was expecting or hoping for one thing—a committed relationship—but what I was communicating to them through what I said and did was the exact opposite. I was keeping things light and casual, thinking that wouldn't "scare them off," but I found out later they thought I wasn't into them.

After that realization, my next relationship was much more honest and open. Even though it didn't work out for other reasons, we still love and support each other as dear friends, which is not something I can say for the rest of my exes before that point. Things shift even when all you do is look at and acknowledge your part in the exchange.

TJ Harvey, Fortune 100 pharmaceutical executive, had to take a hard look at a situation she found herself in very early in her career in the pharmaceutical industry and it turned into an important pivotal moment for her. Less than a year into a job, she'd had about enough of her manager's dismissive and devaluing manner and finally decided to get it off her chest. When they finally met, TJ told her manager that her goal was to leave her office feeling as good about herself as she did when she walked in. The manager was shocked and couldn't understand why TJ felt that way. TJ explained, "'I gave you way too much power in how it made me feel—and today is my day to take that back. I no longer am giving you that power over how I feel about myself, because I've come to the realization that I do actually know what I'm doing. I am kind of smart, and I really should be valued. If you don't see that, then it's just not a good fit.' From that point on, we had an incredible working relationship. . . . It was that moment I stepped into my big girl shoes."

I told TJ that was a "red bottom" moment (as in Louboutin, a luxury brand known for its red-bottomed shoes), because when you step into some Louboutins and you walk up, even if it's figuratively in your mind, that's standing on it. The thing I loved most about her story was that she acknowledged the part she played, just as we had discussed. Communication is a two-way street, even when it's up–down, and even when you have to speak truth to power. TJ helped that manager become a better leader by being a better employee.

Live It comes down to knowing and believing your value proposition (chapter 2) as TJ so perfectly showed us: Who are you? What are you here to do? What do you have to offer? How are those things important to you? You are an expression of many identities and experiences, and every time you connect with others, you bring all those things—along with what you believe and feel about them—to the table. Whether or not you disclose any of those things specifically, you carry all those things with you into every exchange. The specifics may not be anyone's business but what *is* your business is understanding that your perspective is different from everybody else's in the room, and its impact—one of those identities, one of those experiences, one of those viewpoints—can make a difference, and that changes something.

TJ is a firm believer in that impact, that everyone matters. "I think it's so important for people to build awareness for a greater appreciation for how people think, what makes them them, how to get the best out of an organization . . . because when you're getting diversity of thought, diversity of experiences, diversity of looking at the business differently, you are going to bring innovation, new ideas, challenging status quo, really thinking about how you can do things, how you can be a disruptor, quite frankly, in your business."

When diversity comes up in business settings, the focus is usually on representation. Diverse representation is important, but only if we're all free to bring the diversity of thought that comes with our different identities and lived experiences. If all the people in an organization only express themselves in the same codified way that supports the existing culture of an organization, then the true benefit of diversity is lost. It's just different-looking versions of the same thought process, and that completely misses the richness of creativity and innovation that comes from people of all backgrounds expressing their relevant authentic experiences and the added business value that often follows from that. It's an opportunity cost that isn't easy to see until it has already passed or become a liability.

That's a huge benefit of authenticity in the workplace. When people bring their unique experiences and expression to bear on their work, it often serves others in powerful ways and changes lives. I once conducted a leadership training where I worked with an immigrant woman. She had been a client of the organization before becoming an employee, and was incredibly passionate about her job because she sees herself in the people she assists. She told me that as she worked with her team, instead of harsh corrections, she gently nudged them toward understanding why people have the reactions that they do. She shared that they may be scared the INS (Immigration and Naturalization Service) would be notified, or they may not be confident with their command of the language, so they may not understand what was being said. Instead, they'll try to write it down so they can show it to someone who might understand it better with crucial information possibly being lost or misconstrued. If agents had a better facility for their language, she told them, or understood what their concern was, agents could answer them immediately and have an instant impact on their lives.

She was hesitant to speak up with supervisors because English was not her native language and she second-guessed herself when doing presentations. I told her that what she thought was a liability because it was different was also a benefit because it's what helped her advocate for her clients and understand nuances that her colleagues missed. It was why she had achieved as much as she had and was selected for leadership training. She just had to find her own voice and belief in herself to express what she thought needed to be done.

I, in turn, told her supervisors: "I don't know how much you're tapping into this woman, but she *is* your client. She knows instinctively what your clients do that other colleagues might not." I suggested they talk with her about how she's improved the client experience. I couldn't let such a beneficial opportunity for the organization be overlooked.

When you are passionate about something, it will get people's attention. To hold that attention takes your work toward your goals in your passion. It starts when you figure it out and know your value (back to those questions we asked in chapter 2). It's an ongoing process. When you look at yourself closely, you start to see new things that you may not have noticed before. It's like that exercise where you close one eye and then close the other eye, and you'll see something different.

It doesn't happen overnight. It's like peeling an onion, seeing your different layers and realizing that what you do, say, or think *is* important and all the things you have to offer can feed others and, perhaps more importantly, will feed your own soul. That's how you build a career and a life that mean something to you. If you like something about yourself, you're going to highlight it. It's human nature.

No matter where you are on your journey—from first job to experienced leader, from first presentation to skilled speaker—we can all get better at making connections with others. No matter where you are on any spectrum, you can always get better at what you do. I believe connecting authentically is at the core of our success in all walks of life. Even if you're painfully shy or extraordinarily uncomfortable approaching people, you will find a comfortable range where you can operate differently. It could be that you're uncomfortable with a particular type of people and you find a way around them. For a time.

However, our world is getting to a point where there are fewer places to hide and fewer people you can hide behind—as a leader, as a person—and don't ever think you can hide forever. At some point, you're gonna have to talk to somebody about something. And I want you to be able to express yourself well and really connect when you do. There will be at least one moment, probably many of them, when you need to say something that really matters to you, that's high stakes, make-or-break—about your present or future, your family or the love of your life, your business or career—and I want you to be able to say that one thing and know how it will land when you say it. Some things are hard to say, some people are hard to say things to . . . I've hit my mark with many things I've said in my life, but I've also missed the mark completely at a few crucial moments and lost opportunities with friends, loved ones, and in work, all because I avoided saying hard things when I wasn't sure how to say them or I was just plain scared. I've had to live with—and finally let go of—the regrets that go with that, and I'll never miss one of those moments again. We should all sing the song that's in our heart as best we can and never die with our music still inside us. And that's why I do this work now and share what I've learned.

How you connect through effective communication has an enormous impact on your life, career, and in creating relationships of all kinds. You might have an idea, process, or product that could change your work environment, community, or even the world, but first you have to get someone else to understand and believe in it the way you do. That's why I always start with *Live It*—because it all starts with you.

BE BRAVE & BE FREE
AUTHENTICITY ACTIONS

BE BRAVE: It's hard to face yourself, but it's time to test Intention vs. Perception: Is what you intended to say/communicate what the audience perceived?

From your **Record, Review, Refine** session, ask yourself these three questions to determine how you received your message overall when you look at it from the audience's perspective:

- Was it what you intended?

- What did you hear yourself say?

- What can you change to bring the difference between number one and number two closer together? Is that change within your range of authentic expression?

BE FREE: Give yourself permission to make mistakes and don't judge yourself for making them. Only observe how your message affects you and release anything else.

CHAPTER 5

Tell It

MAKE YOUR WORDS MEMORABLE

N ow, let's add on the second foundation for success: *Tell It.*
It all comes down to the power of our stories. Our
words have the potential to draw people in—to share our
experience, create a connection, or even change an outcome. In his book *Actual Minds, Possible Worlds,* cognitive
psychologist Jerome Bruner suggests we are twenty-two times
more likely to remember a fact when it has been wrapped
in a story. For example, if I were to ask you to tell me what's
on your grocery list without looking at it, you'd be pretty
hard-pressed to share more than a few items. But I bet you
remember that embarrassing story your favorite uncle told
about your mama at a family dinner when you were a kid.
Why is that story so much more durable than your grocery
list of stuff you actually need? Because Uncle Joe made you
laugh. He made you feel something. He made you see your
mother in a different light, as a human being, as a young

woman, not just your mama. She had a whole life before you showed up, and now you want to know more. That's the power of stories.

To make facts stick and get people to remember your ideas, weave them into a story. This goes back to the time before humans had easy access to the written word, when all we had was what we said—oral history. Once we learned to talk, we still didn't have books. So, somebody had to keep all the important information in their head: where to find food, what animals were dangerous, why people shouldn't go out of the cave at night. They shared these stories on repeat as new people came into their communities. And people remembered them over the years, because if they didn't, it could mean life or death. Stories may not mean life or death as much anymore and there are certainly far more of them flying around thanks to advances in technology, but they're still one of the most significant ways for humans to share information. Our job now is to make our stories stand out amid the competition for people's attention so they will remember what we have to say.

Everybody experiences stories differently, and there are various ways to construct a story. It doesn't have to be a narrative. You don't have to tell it in chronological order. How you do it is your business. Telling a story is the point. Putting information into context is what stories do. If your presentation is full of numbers or stats, context is what makes them useful and noteworthy. Paint a picture so others can visualize what you're saying, evoke an emotion they can relate to, answer a question they want answered, appeal to what they care about, and show what's in it for them. Those elements create connection and make you and what you're sharing memorable. Your authentic expression shares your value without you ever having to state what it is out loud. People will sit up, take notice, and want to know more about you and whatever you're talking about.

I'm a big believer in using the story construction that fits your purpose. Find inspiration in culturally specific ways of communicating. One of my favorite storytelling structures I grew up hearing is common in Black American culture—starting a story with what might be considered the traditional ending. We share the important stuff first: "Girl, he got married!" and then we tell you how it happened. I think that's a good setup for a business story: "We reached our goal!" Then explain how it was achieved and how you can do it again. Everybody's on board because you already told them what they needed to hear and everybody loves to win. Your colleagues care about the results.

But you might be thinking: *What if we weren't successful? How do I tell that story?* Look at what they care about: "We came within 80 percent of our goal. Here's why we got that far and how we do things differently next time to achieve that last 20 percent." Focus on the solution; give them information they can act on. If you only have a couple minutes to speak or your audience has a short attention span, keep it short and tell them what they care about most and what they can do to achieve success.

A story can be anything you want it to be. Look at top-grossing movies such as *Barbie, Knives Out,* or *Titanic*: it doesn't matter where the story starts or how many people are telling it, as long as it grabs the audience and serves their needs (more on this in chapter 6). It also helps to use mental pictures so your audience can actually see what you're talking about. By offering detailed images, people can create a scene in their mind—like when you're reading a book and you invent this whole world in your head. This allows your audience to build a stronger connection to what you're saying because they're creating something in their mind that's related. Like, I could just tell you I'm sitting under a tree and you'll have a vague image in your mind, maybe your favorite oak tree. But if I tell you I'm sitting under a palm tree in Hawaii or resting against a cypress tree in Louisiana—now you really can see where I am, because it puts you in a specific place. Or if I'm on a marketing team and tell them that our ad for a client was successful, everyone in the room is imagining a different type of ad and a different measure of success. But if I tell them our email campaign was smash with an open rate of 30 percent and a click-through rate of 10 percent, everyone is on the same page. Specificity is key. You want to help people visualize the scene in their minds to make it, as Jason DeSanto, my colleague from Northwestern University, said, "sticky." That stickiness comes from the audience's participation in a mental activity with the specific information we're giving them.

People won't remember facts and figures if you fail to put them in context. They will end up assuming whatever they want about the numbers unless you appeal to what they care about and weave a narrative around that. Your interpretation is power because it directs the audience/listeners toward a conclusion or an action you'd like them to take as a result of your story. Don't rely on a chart or diagram. Make it all make sense—with words. I know, I know, that's all easier said than done in a business situation. You *know* your boss, team, and client may not have much time or patience for a narrative.

But if you shape the information you have to tell in a way that's interesting, meaningful, and puts it into context, you'll make it sticky. You could define a problem, offer a solution or a plan by telling the story of where you are now, what needs fixing, and how you're going to fix it. Or you could tell the story of how you got to this point and where you're heading next. Slide your facts and figures into the story to support key points and you're done!

One of my clients was charged with delivering new messaging for his organization on their purpose to the community. At the time, equitable transit-oriented development (eTOD) was a newer concept in city planning and development centered around existing public transportation instead of highways and driving. It was technical and interdisciplinary, encompassing everything from transit to construction to social justice, so it wasn't easy to explain or grasp. But when he started thinking in terms of why the work was important to him personally—making sure that the resources available in cities were accessible to all its residents—and connecting that to sharing stories of their successes in communities where their projects had already made neighborhoods more walkable and given community members better transit options to reach their jobs, it became much easier for people who had never heard of this kind of work to understand and support what they were doing. He found the way to easily digest what he was talking about—he got buy-in through his stories. When that revelation happens, the audience will likely ask for more data or details so they can look deeper into the problem or project. You've got to give them a little something extra that makes them want more. That's the hook.

What makes something a hook? Anything that carries the emotion the audience cares about: What's in it for me? What's in it for the people I care about? What's memorable? Think about the best memories you've ever had. There's usually a strong emotion tied to them. You will pull your audience right in if you attach an emotion to your story. In business situations, you could use the emotion of excitement over sales, relief that you hit your numbers, or satisfaction with a job well done.

Many of us try to take emotions out of the equation, especially when we're in the office (or on Zoom), but as human beings, it doesn't usually work. We forget that the only reason anybody does anything is because of how they feel about it—positive or negative. Am I doing this so that I can be a star employee (recognition)? Am I doing it because I'm afraid of what will happen if I don't do it? Am I going to lose something if I don't do this? FOMO? Fear is a big motivator. I don't like it as a motivator because fear only gives us enough gas to avoid whatever pain or discomfort we're experiencing; the motivation from fear alone doesn't usually last long enough to generate or create anything new, solid, or enduring. But it's someplace to start.

While we're on the topic of motivation, I want to clarify what your stories cannot do, and that's motivate someone to do something. *Merriam-Webster* defines *motivate* as: to provide with a motive. In turn, *motive* means: something (as a need or desire) that causes a person to act. By its very definition, motivation is internal. No one can know better than us what's going to get us up off our butts and actually do something.

Don't get me wrong. I understand why people love to use that word. It's an action word, a strong verb, and when you turn it into a noun or an adjective, it becomes very power-ful. I'm probably splitting hairs here and being very partic-ular about language, but it's important for me to be precise in using language when it comes to how we speak to one another (and ourselves).

I find that when people tell their stories, they most often want to be motivational, but don't understand what that takes. It takes inspiration, which is a much better goal for our stories to strive to be. *Merriam-Webster* defines *inspirational* as: the action or power of moving the intellect or emotions, and *inspire* means: to spur on or to affect. So, what we mean when we want to be motivational is we want to impact someone with our words and move their minds or hearts. Isn't that a much easier task? Consider what emotions move or inspire you and how you can transmit those emotions to others in a way that moves them to act. Now, that's a good story!

Emotions are tricky, though. They always leak out some-how, and the more you try to suppress them, the more they want to be expressed. But here's the thing—emotions create connections between people, especially in stories. The speci-ficity of your story paints a picture for them, and their brain is engaged. They feel the emotions and, if they're shared, form an attachment. Then, from the narrative, they get a sense that you can solve problems. If they've got that prob-lem now or in the future, they're coming to you because you provided a solution and communicated the story of that solution, which leads to building a relationship and the con-nection in their brain back to you, because you told them a story about it.

Emotion is the reason passionate leaders are often most effective in getting people to follow them. Controversial though they are, I believe it's a big part of the reason President Donald Trump and Elon Musk have been so successful. Regardless of their message, people respond to the ethos around it.

RHETORIC REVISITED

If we go back to rhetoric or what classical speaking is—the appeals are pathos, logos, and ethos.

Pathos, or the appeal to emotions, means to persuade an audience to feel a certain way, like angry or sympathetic.

Logos, or the appeal to logic, means to appeal to the audience's sense of reason or logic.

Ethos, or the appeal to authority and credibility, means convincing an audience of the reliable character of the speaker/writer.

The best speakers in the world all express a distinct ethos: President Barack Obama, Dr. Martin Luther King Jr., President John F. Kennedy, British prime minister Margaret Thatcher, evangelist Billy Graham, Oprah Winfrey, Maya Angelou, British prime minister Winston Churchill. Their power is in their identity and essence—their *Fearless Authenticity,* if you will—because that's what they've shared with us through their speaking. Their appeal goes beyond just the logic or reasoning (logos) they've shared or how any emotion (pathos) they've expressed made us feel. It's all those things and the trust we have in them that makes us follow them and hang on to every well-crafted, expertly delivered word.

Knowing this is true, why would we ever take emotion out of what we do at work? What actually gets us to do something is how we *feel* about it, how passionate we are. Most leaders people follow are the ones who are passionate about what they do. They may have a whole lot of logic that they dispense along with it, but they're fierce in their beliefs and they speak to something that strikes a chord in those who follow them.

I know I said a story can take any form you want, but it has to have some kind of structure or your audience won't be able to follow you and they'll give up. Some of the best options I've found for constructing a strong narrative focus on a few important elements. First off, think about what you're offering. Focus on that and make sure it's at least three things—this is true of facts, questions, information, but most of all, choices. When given only two options, people will belabor and deliberate longer, most likely because it feels like one answer must be right and the other wrong. But there's something about odd numbers that's comforting and memorable—if you offer three or even five, there's always a clear winner; plus lists of three or five things are just easier to remember. More on that in a bit.

Next, design your story with a beginning, middle, and end. As I mentioned earlier, you can start wherever you like—for example, at the end, then go back to the beginning or even the middle. The most important element, especially in functional stories that serve a purpose (in your work, for instance), is having some sort of closure to your story, or even better, something for your listener to do or look forward to. A call to action or a tease of what's to come can be extremely powerful in getting and keeping your audience's interest.

Regardless of the structure you use, your goal is to always make it memorable. Take a step back if you need to and make sure you have something to say that's worth remembering. Trust between speaker and audience is paramount—don't waste the audience's time. My favorite method to make something memorable goes back to the earliest joke structure from the vaudeville era (staged entertainment popular in the early twentieth century and the precursor to what we know as stand-up comedy today):

1. First, tell the audience you're going to tell them a joke.
2. Then, you tell them the joke.
3. Finally, you tell them that you told them the joke.

This is part of the reason we repeat good punch lines ("that's what *she* said!"). It's what we remember and it's what we *want* them to remember. That's what is so powerful about this structure—the repetition. People need repetition to remember, especially when they're listening to something (as opposed to reading, watching, or doing). Marketing research shows the average person needs to hear a message seven times before they take action. Every impression (instance of someone seeing/hearing something) makes it more memorable.

If you're doing a presentation or explaining a complex problem, you hope that your audience is primed to listen and interested in what you have to say. Even then, it's still a great idea to reinforce what you want to stick in their brains. To use this structure for a speech:

> **Intro:** These are the things I want you to pay attention to.
>
> **Body:** These are the things to pay attention to.
>
> **Close:** These are the things I wanted you to pay attention to.

To further that stickiness, one way to wrap up your presentation is by telling the audience exactly what you want them to keep in mind: "If you don't remember anything else I said today, remember this."

We use our stories to answer questions. It's usually one of the Five Ws, a journalism standard: Who, What, Where, When, and Why (and sometimes How). "Why" is the hardest to answer, because there's no definitive answer to it and it can be difficult to pin down. "Why" changes depending on who you ask. It could also represent a challenge to a belief or turn into a defense or justification of a belief. It's not just an invitation to dialogue; it could mean a fight. It's the least predictable of all the questions, a wild card. So, if you want to find out why, substitute "in what way," and go a little gentler with it.

And when you're preparing a presentation that will likely include some kind of visuals—slides, video, or diagram—people/audiences always want more pictures than words. It's more engaging for somebody to look at a video of you talking than for them to read a post that you wrote or to read graphics. This applies whether you're in person, on social media, or on TV. But if all you have is your voice, like radio or a podcast, you'd better talk in pictures. About 65 percent of the population are visual learners, while around 30 percent learn best through hearing. And in case you're wondering, the last 5 percent are kinesthetic—they learn by doing.

Regardless, translating what you say into something visual is absolutely necessary. You have to give people a picture. It's just like when you're reading a book, you get engaged with the story when you imagine what's in it. Same thing with audiobooks: If somebody's explaining something and they're painting a picture, then you get attached because it becomes your picture. You're invested in the story because you've created something that connects to it—just for you.

BRING THE DRAMA!

I said it doesn't matter how you tell a story. But one thing that will make your story compelling and memorable is drama. Human beings love drama, or, more specifically, we love seeing conflict and resolution. It's cathartic, a release; maybe it even brings closure. And it's as true in your work as it is on your favorite TV show—every work problem holds a conflict looking for a resolution.

The most effective way to create an incredible picture in your audience's mind is to lean into how you feel about the message you are spreading. Let the emotion come through. If you're an engineer, and you're describing how a widget works, something obviously inspired you to make it. Why? That's what people want to know. In a lot of ways, you get to the "what's in it for me" through "what's in it for you?" What inspired you? That inspiration is what you craft your message around. What is the story you're trying to tell? What is the emotion? What is the essence, the nugget that's going to be appealing to people? Identify that and make sure that it's infused in everything you say. It answers what people care about; what drew you to the idea in the first place.

Chicago TV reporter and anchor Jackie Kostek knows the power of crafting a strong story that appeals to people's emotions. One of the most powerful stories she's told is her own, about her hair loss and the devastation she felt. "I really thought my life was over . . . I couldn't see a way past it," she told me. But, over time, she had a new realization. "I had everything that I had before, except for hair, and once I found a hairpiece that looks natural and worked for me, there was nothing that was gonna really hold me back."

Getting to that point didn't happen overnight. It took time and lots of patience waiting—on herself. She told me, "I think, for me, it was waiting until I really felt the self-love come up from it, where . . . it wasn't going to make me cry every single time I talked about it." She recalled the moment that happened: "I was really starting to feel that shift on the anchor desk, and I would get home at night, take off the hairpiece . . . I would wash off my face and just stare at myself in the mirror. And I'm like, how the hell did I do this? . . . I was so proud of myself . . . And I was, like, you did that, like you somehow have made this life for yourself."

She hopes to share her story with more women to show them it's possible to live a full life with it (or any body issue). "I think there's such power because every woman who is fearlessly authentic in their lives has probably had a moment like that where you've been brought to your knees and made to question just about everything in your life."

While you may be hesitant to tell a personal story during a presentation or team meeting or Instagram Live or, in Jackie's case, live on television, it's a powerful way to make a connection, convey who you are and your expectations for others, and build stronger relationships.

"The more stories I told, the more I felt the power of my own story . . . I was like, no, I shouldn't be afraid of it . . . I want the story to be given a platform and exposure just to see if it can help a few other women in their journey."

I'm so proud of Jackie for learning this early in her career. When I was at the point she is, I always hesitated to share details of my personal life on-air. I was always very private, especially about my romantic life. From my perspective, I wanted to be respectful to my partners because we were dating and not married; they didn't sign up for public scrutiny. I did open up to my listeners when my mama died, but only because I needed to share it to get back to work; it was how I dealt with my grief. And even then, with no social media, I received support from my fans—they were grieving with me.

As the industry has changed, with reality television and media platforms expanding into every part of our lives, the level of revelation you need to share is staggering, because people want to know more, to connect with you. Just look at Taylor Swift. She lives her life under a microscope, every moment scrutinized. But in turn, Taylor has not been afraid to open up about her vulnerabilities and struggles, creating a bond with her fans and building a much stronger audience.

Celebrity author Glennon Doyle built her audience similarly, talking about her experiences honestly, not just the "Instagram" of things, but showing her authenticity through her stories, and even more so with her podcast. When I sat down to interview her, I had no idea she would change my whole outlook on the work of being fearless. I saw the power in telling the whole truth, not holding back or being selective as I had been doing. Talking with her was a turning point for me. Afterward, I opened up on-air about being my dad's caregiver and even told my listeners I was having a hysterectomy. Being fearless to share my struggles expanded my comfort level and brought another layer of realness to my work and a stronger connection to my viewers. You never know how your story will resonate with people when you're fully honest and transparent.

There is a range, though, of where certain things are appropriate or comfortable for you. I call it the *elasticity of authenticity*. You have to find the balance between what you disclose, when, to whom, and for what reason. One of my favorite examples of this was when I was working in morning TV. Our team was brainstorming about autism awareness and how we could best present a story. After we'd been talking for a while, not quite taking the right approach, one of our producers spoke up. She has two autistic children and shared her thoughts. Not everyone knew about her kids, so she took a real chance and said: "Listen, this is our experience. This is how we should be talking about this." And she was careful to only talk about what her kids experience and admitted she didn't know everything, but suggested a way for us to start so that our coverage was much more sensitive. Imagine if she had chosen to stay silent. We could have offended our viewers and embarrassed ourselves. Her willingness to speak up shows how bringing our experiences and knowledge to the table can make real change.

The other piece is that she didn't have to tell us it was her experience. If she didn't feel comfortable talking about her own children, she could have just said, "Gang, I know a little something about this, and I think we're going in the wrong direction." She still could have shared her experience without qualifying it because she didn't have to. It was her choice. Some people object to authenticity in the workplace: the "I don't want them telling me about their whole family" thing. You don't have to. But if you have that experience, can't you make somebody else's experience richer by sharing something you know? It's all in how you choose to do it. If you aren't comfortable around a certain group of people, don't share with them. Trust that feeling. If it's something you're passionate about, find a way to bring in your perspective. You could offer to take over a project, because you can influence it in a different way. That's what I mean about the range of authenticity. I think a lot of times people think authenticity is just disclosure. It's so much more than that.

My former morning show cohost Melissa Forman was never afraid to bring her home life to work. Every day during our broadcast, she shared stories about her husband and four children, unfiltered and full of lessons and laughs. I asked her one time what made her feel safe to be that vulnerable.

"Number one, I'm born and raised here," she said with certainty. "So, I feel very comfortable that these are the people that I grew up with. But I also feel like it goes back to that idea that the truth always comes out . . . I don't really have anything to hide with you. I'll tell you the good, the bad, the ugly, whatever. My life is imperfect . . . I just realized early on, why hide from it, just share who you are, and open it up, and celebrate the good and bad. And that's what's relatable. . . . That's what we're doing here. We're sharing our lives."

Melissa perfectly sums up why words matter and sharing stories matters even more. They can convey who you are, what you expect, and what others can expect of you. Their power lies in how we put the facts and pieces of our work/life experiences together in a way that makes meaning for others . . . which creates connection. And everything we could possibly want flows from there—to lead, to have an impact, to be successful—which is just our current culture's way to be remembered and to matter ourselves.

BE BRAVE, BE FREE, BE YOU
AUTHENTICITY ACTION

Can people identify with your story—does it leave them feeling something?

Test Your *Tell It*.

Write down examples of people connecting with your story.

When you can *Be Brave* enough to share your story, and *Be Free* enough to leave in and share the emotions of what happened, that's when you can fully *Be You*. That opens the door for us to connect with each other.

CHAPTER 6

Sell It

USE YOUR WORDS TO SERVE

My Foundation for Success number three: *Sell It.*

Everybody is always selling something. If you're thinking, *Wait, I'm not in sales,* think again. Listen, I understand why you feel this way. It took me twenty-some years of my career to realize I have been selling for my entire life. I know! I was just as shocked as you. How could I not recognize it? That's all any of us do, right? Sales is indeed a job, but we don't have to be in sales to sell something. We're selling ourselves, whether we're trying to convince somebody what restaurant to go to, what to cook for dinner, or where we should go on vacation. The things we want in life are usually things we pitch or sell to someone else: seeking support for an idea, persuading someone to take action, convincing a company to hire us, or getting someone to buy our product.

WHAT I MEAN BY AUDIENCE

Every last one of us has an audience, no matter who we're connecting with—one person on social media, your family at dinner, thirty people in a conference room, or hundreds of thousands of viewers online. Your message means nothing without an audience to hear it. And owning the power of knowing your audience is how you make sure it's heard.

Your audience, depending on the context, may be clients, customers, buyers, or prospects; in other situations, they're your colleagues, coworkers, or team; it could be your manager, boss, supervisor, or CEO; you might even call them stakeholders, partners, or collaborators; or perhaps spouse, partner, child, parent, or friend. No matter how many of them are gathered together, from one to thousands, the people who care about what you do are your audience.

Who cares about what you do?

To connect with people and make "the sale," whatever it may be, here are the three questions I want you to ask yourself every single time:

1. Who are they?
2. Why do they care?
3. How can I serve them?

When I say *who are they*, it is not about demographics. It is about who they are as people, because that leads you to the next question—*Why do they care?*

My former morning show cohost and dear friend Melissa Forman was notorious for shouting in our post-show meetings "Why does *she* care?" when we discussed potential segments or guests. Our audience was mainly women. Melissa would say again and again: "Don't waste her time! Only give her something she cares about—is *this* really what she cares about?!"

Another way to look at that question is: Why *should* they care? As the saying goes, you don't know what you don't know. A good portion of selling someone on something new is letting them know about it first, then giving them a reason they should care about it.

When we have something to say, our focus is often solely on the message we want to deliver. That's a crucial element certainly, as is asking yourself this question: What do they need/want to hear about that I have to share with them? Once you understand why they care, you can start building relationships, because that's what this is all about—making connections. Especially, *How can I serve them?* It's not about pleasing them. It's about providing what people need that they can't get for themselves—that you already have. That's how you cement that bond.

Many times when we talk about audiences, we primarily think about demographics. We distill people down to numbers, and we don't look too far past that. Marketers call this *psychographics*. It's just getting to know them—the story about what those numbers might tell you about people beyond their age, gender, and race. Generationally, millennials have a storyline; boomers definitely have a history, along with Gen Xers (as ignored as we feel sometimes) and Gen Z. Their lives are made up of more than their stats, like age, gender, race, education level, occupation, or marital status. It's what's behind those identities that really matters: What does "female" or "gender nonconforming" mean for that person? Or being Black, brown, Asian, or Native American? How about being a parent, grandparent, or sibling? Or being gay, straight, or asexual? Or a caregiver, an immigrant, or a person with disabilities? When we use demographics, such as women ages twenty-five to fifty-four, we have to consider all the underlying factors that make up individuals—what impacts their life. For example:

- Are they having trouble with aging?

- Do they live alone?

- Do they have pets?

- Are they parents?

- Do they struggle with mental health?

- Do they like their job?

- Do they have a religious affiliation?

The list goes on and on. Knowing people beyond the numbers is what makes them real. The more you know about them, the more you know what they care about and why they would or should care about what you're talking about.

My former boss and radio mentor Elroy Smith used to hammer home that we had to overserve our core audience.

They're the people who ride or die with you, no matter what—your best supporters. His theory is if we overserve them by giving them everything they want from a radio station, their enthusiasm for what they get will spread to their friends, family, and acquaintances and our audience would grow organically—authentically.

When you start to think about your audience as someone or a group you serve, like a satellite you are orbiting around, that expands your focus from what you want to say to what will best serve them. Your audience always cares about something—usually a problem they need your help to solve.

Arlan Hamilton, founder of Backstage Capital, created her venture fund business to help solve the problem of funding disparities in tech for people of color, women, and/or LGBTQIA+ (she identifies as all three). When I spoke with her at the 2022 Grace Hopper Celebration of Women in Computing, she shared the simple but perceptive way she connects with her audience: "Be who you are so people looking for you can find you." She said she made a commitment to being her true authentic self so she could attract "her people." That doesn't mean they all look like her or come from the same background. She said, "There's a compass that's leading them to me and me to them."

For me, that's what the *Fearless Authenticity* piece is—understand the value that you have and trust that it will guide you to your people, even if you don't know who they all are yet. You know some of them, perhaps many of them, but get to know them better. What do they care about, what do they need, what do they want, what is it that you have that can serve them? There's always more to know . . . and that knowledge may be the thing that helps you discover how to serve them better . . . and convince them to buy whatever it is you're selling..

The most straightforward way to find out what they want or need is to ask questions. Make sure the questions are pointed and useful to get the information you need. Author and movie critic Matt Pais has some of the best advice I've ever heard on the topic: "The quality of the answers is often very much proportional to the quality of the questions." In his work reviewing movies, he's interviewed many celebrities. He learned early on that if he didn't start with great questions, he would get the transcription back and hear a bunch of boring generalities. Then he was stuck with absolutely nothing to work with. Same goes for gaining insight into whom you're serving—decide what you want to know about them, what connections you want to make, and what knowledge will get you there. Be curious.

Curiosity and a sense of discovery—which requires you to stay flexible and open—are as important, if not more important, as anticipating what your audience needs or wants. Even when you approach your inquiry with due diligence, you can still make assumptions, create problems that don't exist, or miss the things that really need addressing. If you get too attached to what you already believe, then you're always going to be wrong. Okay, maybe not all the time—a stopped clock is right twice a day, as the saying goes. While you might be right a decent percentage of the time, you're going to miss the little nuances that truly define your audience and that could prevent you from finding, connecting with, and understanding your people. That's what we're really talking about. Find the match between the people you think are your audience and the people who really are receptive to what you have to say. You may want to reach certain people, but you may also reach somebody else that you didn't expect to. When you make that discovery, it's time to shift and make it work for you. And them.

A good example of this is what happens in most TV markets around the country. In Chicago, there are four main network stations plus several independent stations vying for number one in TV ratings. Everyone wants that top spot. I've seen it happen time and again—a station that's in fourth place or lower starts chasing the first-place station's audience and abandons or doesn't appreciate the audience it already has. Often, that top station is dominant because they found the right mix of what they do and who they serve and they keep doing it. And they overserve, as Elroy preached, their core audience. The only way you chip away at their lead is by finding a subset of that group that isn't being fully served by them and serving them to grow your audience and rise to number three, then number two as you get ready to face off for number one. Here's the thing—why would you chase someone else's audience if you have found your people and you're doing well? You will end up ticking off the people who love you just to get the people who only like you.

Once you discover what your audience needs, you can communicate your value in helping them reach their goal and establish lasting relationships with them. This is how you differentiate yourself and create a more durable relationship, especially if your product is a commodity or you have a lot of competition. People make decisions based on relationships. That will be your advantage.

My daddy used to say if you're gonna spend money, you may as well do it with someone you like. Think about it. You will follow a hairstylist or barber around town or drive out of your way to a dry cleaner or bakery because you like how they take care of you. You've made a connection. You feel a belonging. In today's world, we focus a lot on differences because they make us unique and define who we are and how we relate to one another. But there's more commonality in who we are than we're often willing to acknowledge.

Former *Chicago Tribune* syndicated columnist Heidi Stevens doesn't shy away from writing about her own personal struggles surrounding her divorce, remarriage, parenting, stepparenting, and more. She told me that by admitting her stumbles, she "could just publicly be human, and not a character who tries to be flawless . . . and that's the way it would help people feel less alone. I tried to seek out stories that would help people feel less lonely by saying here's someone else who may be a bereaved mom, and what that looks like and feels like to her . . . or here's somebody who stepped up and helped a neighbor, maybe that's something you'd want to model, stories that kind of connected us again."

She looks at it as a way to help people figure out where they belong, which is what we all want.

"You might have people around you, but you don't feel like you belong there," she said. "You feel like you're not what those people want you to be, but to become more of what those people want you to be would betray you and your own principles or heart or integrity."

Heidi's theory about being true to yourself gets at the heart of *Fearless Authenticity*. We all have roles in life; all these things that we are expected to do. Sometimes we confuse the roles we take on, are assigned, and play in others' lives with who we really are. Yes, we may be parents, siblings, children, spouses, teachers, lawyers, doctors, and so on. We can fulfill our duties in those roles and enjoy them while we do that, but we will never just be those roles, and any one of them will never be all of who we are, no matter how important they are to us. We find our true power in how we fulfill our purpose through each of the roles we choose to inhabit, doing them as no one else possibly could.

I intentionally include the word *serve* in the last question of *Sell It*: How can I serve them? It's why I believe we're all here: to serve one another with the gifts we've been given. Our highest calling, regardless of what we do, is that all of us serve a purpose for other people. It's just a matter of figuring out what that purpose is, and then infusing everything we do with that purpose, on purpose. Our actions have so much more power when we do them with intention.

I saw this happen when I hosted morning television—it's a perfect example of how your path to success opens up when you discover your purpose. It's one of my favorite success stories. Jocelyn Delk Adams is the founder, best-selling author, national TV personality, and brand ambassador behind Grandbaby Cakes. When we first met, her baking blog was just starting to take off. She was working full-time as a TV production assistant and making cakes at night in her one-bedroom apartment.

"I was really unsure exactly what I wanted to do," she shared. "I kept just going back to the kitchen when I wanted to find myself . . . I was baking my grandmother's recipes . . . I was constantly baking cakes for friends and family. I realized it's where I'm most happy. It's where I feel the most fulfilled. And there was this sense of connection . . . I wanted to share the story of the recipes that my grandmother gifted me with and that legacy and move that into people's homes. So, it was a different way of connecting."

Friends suggested she open a bakery, but Jocelyn knew that life wasn't for her. "I don't think that's my ministry," she told me. "I don't want to be up at three o'clock in the morning, constantly churning it out."

Jocelyn said what helped her find her authentic self was to gather a group of women together to support one another on their journey, figuring out what they wanted to do. Her path became clear to her when she was baking for friends. She told a member of her support group that she was feeling burned out baking for people constantly.

"I need to figure out a way where I can still be creative, still connect with people, and also share the recipes," and that's when her friend suggested writing a blog.

"It was like the first moment of having the electric impulse," she said, "where I was like, 'Oh my gosh, this is so exciting.' I'm working nine to five, but every night I was rushing home to work on a new blog post or shoot new recipes. It was all very new and fresh but very exciting."

Her best advice if you're struggling to find your purpose is to identify your support group—people who are going through the same thing and will have your back. She also recommends trying a lot of different things to see what sticks. I would add to that the advice I gave interns when they asked me about getting into broadcasting: Say yes until it's a hard no. Say yes to everything. Look past your assumptions about what work you may or may not love and give it all a try. You may be surprised about jobs you think you wouldn't like that turn out to be an absolute yes, because there are things about them you can't see from the outside until you're in that moment.

Once we identify how we can be of service through our work and know where we can have a positive impact, it becomes so much easier to find more ways to replicate and amplify the positive effect we can have in other arenas. At the end of the day, that's what it's really all about. When you *Sell It* with fearless authenticity, you not only serve other people what they want and need, but you get what *you* want and need, too.

When you make these feel-good connections, it might seem like you've achieved something rare. But often, cultivating and keeping those relationships comes down to building chemistry. I do believe there can be instant chemistry between certain people, a kind of magic that happens—like catching lightning in a bottle. But that is not the only kind of chemistry there is. In most situations, chemistry takes work. Whatever kind of chemistry you have with someone—instant or the kind you build—you have to work to keep it alive. Chemistry, as it relates to *Sell It,* is about building trust and rapport to get things done—good working chemistry with others is what helps us find our flow and get where we all want to go.

The first step into that flow is getting intentional in creating the chemistry that allows it to happen. Understand that your brain pays more attention to evidence that supports what you already believe to be true. So, when we have that lightning-in-a-bottle moment with someone, we tend to see all the things we find exciting about that person, thus reinforcing that feeling. We look forward to those things and build on that. When we don't have that lightning-in-a-bottle moment, we think it's not possible to create the spark and instead focus on the things that don't give us that spark as proof. What we forget is that we can train our brains to see anything we want, and create the chemistry we need in any situation to get things done. Here's the way I like to think about it, courtesy of model and TV personality Tyra Banks from an interview we did back when she was starting her show, *America's Next Top Model.* She told me:

"Start with yourself to see how it works: Pick a feature on your face you really like; focus on it and see how much you like it. Once you do that, you'll start to notice something else you like, and then another thing, until you feel better about what you look like, and yourself."

You can do the same thing when you're trying to build rapport and trust with someone to get to a good, working chemistry—and it works whether you don't know each other yet or you're repairing a rocky past. Think of this process as an expansion of the first *Sell It* question, from "Who are they?" to "Who are they, and what do I appreciate or respect about them?" Hone in on a trait you admire about them, instead of something you can't stand or find boring. Concentrate on that quality you value and let that lead your interactions and be the gateway to finding other things you respect, admire, or appreciate. Those things will combine to form a relationship, make a connection, build trust. To me, when there's respect and trust, that's the best kind of chemistry you can have. That's when you can create real magic with somebody. When you find that common ground, what's super valuable about that person, it's going to shift how you treat and how you engage with that person. And it's going to change the quality of your exchanges as you pick up on each other's moods, priorities, or mindsets.

We spend a lot of time looking for chemistry instead of building it. We kind of just want or hope it will happen. Yes, there will be people you'll have better working relationships with or who are easier to deal with. But just like you don't get to pick your family, you don't always get to pick with whom you share an office. If you're having challenges, building some sort of chemistry is helpful. Why? Because we mirror one another all the time. As human beings, it's how we communicate. It's awfully hard not to smile back when someone smiles at you; likewise, it's difficult not to frown back. So, model the behavior you want to see: *This is what I would like. This is what I would like back. Can I get it?* If there's a connection, I'm going to give it to you, period, and hope I get it back. It's not conditional or transactional. But if you want a certain response, you're not going to get it by doing the opposite. It's just not gonna happen that way.

When Melissa and I worked together on our morning show, we talked a lot about how you can have instant chemistry and be a good fit on-air, but it's just like any relationship—you still have to work at it. When you hit those rough patches where things aren't going great, you have to find a way to address it. My approach to building our relationship was what I mentioned above: focus on the thing I loved about Missy, as I was soon calling Melissa.

We had some clashes when we first started as cohosts. It was never any one big thing, just all the little stuff that works on each other's nerves a little, but really adds up when not addressed. I only remember having one actual argument with her and all I remember about it is how bad I felt when it was over because I knew it was petty. All our differences boiled down to our past experiences and inexperience in our current situation—we both were used to being solo performers; we liked to do things our own way and didn't have anyone helping us navigate through the process of becoming partners and a team. However, deep down, we both were looking for a confidant, someone we could share the load with—we just had to find our way to it for each other. I'd always had subordinate roles in my previous work partnerships, so with Missy, I learned how to be a team player on equal footing so we could succeed. Even though we both irritate each other to this day with the same stuff, it's funny to us now, because we got intentional about sharing what we needed, then accepting and understanding how what we did served the other person.

We accomplished a lot of that work through listening to each other and really hearing what each other was saying. So often we're focused on the message we want to deliver instead of what people need to hear about it from us. We often focus only on what we want to say in conversations instead of what the other person is saying. A dialogue is an exchange between two people and that requires listening and responding. Anything less is just a monologue with someone else present.

I often use the example of being in an argument but never hearing what the other person is saying. You're just listening to what they're saying so you can respond with what you want them to hear. I've had this problem, mainly with romantic relationships. While I've had success with it in my work, with my audiences, in friendships, and even family, I used to screw this up every single time with significant others. I know I'm messing it up when I'm doing it. But caring for my dad before he died helped me improve how I listened and responded. I adjusted my *Sell It* questions for our changing relationship to:

- Who are they *now?*

- What do they care about *now?*

- How can I serve them *now?*

I'll be honest, though, it took some time to realize I wasn't practicing what I preached. My daddy and I were being our most fearlessly authentic selves—just not with each other at the beginning of our caregiving journey. Even though I'm decisive in my own life, I resisted being the decision maker in his life because I still saw him as my daddy and didn't want to see how he was declining. And he resisted asking for help except in the most indirect of ways—like waiting until I came home and noticed something needed doing or having my aunt say something to me—all because he didn't want to give up any control over his own life and he still saw himself as responsible for me because I was still his child. We were fully committed to keeping those roles intact until he had a diabetic episode that landed him in the hospital and scared us both into getting real with each other about who we were, what we cared about, and how we could serve that *now.*

Many of my one-on-one clients picked up on my lessons faster than I did. Several have said: "This has made my relationship better. My connection with my children is better because I'm not just telling them what to do or what I need

119

them to hear. If I do have a message I need to give them, I'm taking into account how they need to hear it from me."

Others who came to me for help with their professional communication skills realized that revealing their *Fearless Authenticity* at home helped them better navigate difficult conversations with their (aging) parents, children, partners, coworkers, friends. Why? Because the core of any relationship is communication.

Work relationships can be particularly tough for many people, figuring out how to negotiate conflicts and temper expectations. My colleague Joan, a retired doctor and adjunct professor, admittedly has had a challenging time with people in general, rubbing them the wrong way with her candidness and low tolerance for errors. However, because she is aware of her triggers, she does apologize for her demeanor, especially at work. She told me, "There have been a lot of situations where I have had to go back and say: 'You know what, I didn't say that the way I should have said it. I apologize for hurting your feelings. I still feel this thing. I just regret hurting your feelings.'"

She said, in most situations, people have understood and it's usually the ones who realized that the advice she shared was helpful, regardless of delivery style. She added that everybody doesn't always feel that way, and she accepts the consequences. That's the crux of it—saying what you have to say is always your option—you just have to be willing to acknowledge the results. Joan is operating as her authentic self, becoming better able to understand how others experience her, what relationships she wants to work on in that way, and adjusting to serve them and their shared goals.

You don't have to change who you are to be of service to others. We often assume that to accommodate others means we must sacrifice ourselves. But you can adapt how you present yourself and your message through your delivery without giving up one bit of your authentic self. This is connected to that elasticity of authenticity I talked about in chapter 5, but here, it's about accessing the full range of your authentic expression in various situations or with different people to successfully execute *Sell It*. You set the boundary for what your adaptation to your audience looks like, whether that's choosing not to use profanity when you speak to your grandmother out of respect for her, or choosing to use it when telling a story to your friends at the bar. Making both of those choices could be authentic to you (I know it has been for me and my potty mouth), and doing so doesn't make you any less of who you are. But it certainly affects how both of those audiences hear you.

It all comes down to my favorite Maya Angelou quote: "I've learned that people will forget what you said, people will forget what you did, but people will never forget how you made them feel." At its core, that's how we impact an audience. That's how we become memorable. That's why you go back to the same restaurants or stores, because they're going to take care of you—you may not even know their names, but you know how they make you feel. The same thing happens with the people you interact with: clients, coworkers, colleagues, potential employers, significant others, family members, friends. One of the ways you bring value into someone else's life is how you make that person feel. That's essentially what *Sell It* is all about—creating or shifting dynamics with the people you interact with by seeking to understand who they are, figure out what they care about, and adapt how you reach out to them in a way that's focused on the mutual benefit found in serving them and their needs. Being purposeful and intentional and fearless with all that gives you power.

BE YOU
AUTHENTICITY ACTION

Prepare to *Sell It*.

Ask yourself these three questions about all your audiences:

1. Who are they?

2. Why do they care?

3. How can I serve them?

How do you make them feel? Are you being purposeful?

PART III

FEARLESS AUTHENTICITY IN ACTION

CHAPTER 7

Building Power

Who we are is the gift that we have to give to the world. We have so many roles we play within our families, our workplaces, and our friendships that we often define ourselves by the definitions of those roles. How am I supposed to act as a mother or son; how am I supposed to act as an accountant or as a teacher, a nurse or a TV host? If you behave differently from the norm, you often feel like you don't fit in. You wonder why you're not like that person who's super successful. We get caught up in trying to live up to the ideal of these roles instead of trying to live as the ideal version of our fearlessly authentic selves.

Being your authentic self is how you build your power. There are thousands of accountants in the world; same goes for teachers, nurses, and TV hosts. Those of us who are successful, though, are the ones who do it the way *we* do it. People remember us for the way we do things, good or bad. I once had a bum accountant. He wasn't terrible at his job—he really was excellent—he just wasn't the right person for me. He didn't answer questions the way I needed them to be answered or explained, and he didn't understand why I didn't understand, so we parted ways.

We sometimes get so confused; we think, *I'm supposed to do it a certain way*, especially when we're starting a new career, either just out of school or at midlife. That's why we take classes or go back to school or get credentials. None of that is wrong, it could be exactly what's needed, as long as you don't lose sight of your core because it's the important part of who we are.

As people progress through their careers and get their ten thousand hours in (the number of hours it takes to achieve mastery of complex skills, according to Malcolm Gladwell's rule as explained in his book *Outliers*), they take pride that they've mastered a skill and become experts. They know what they do well and stick to what they know. Which is great, until that one skill and how they currently use it becomes the *only* thing they do with it. That's where they get stuck and their power stops building.

However, there are others, like performers, especially those with long, successful careers like comedy legend George Wallace, who build on their expertise by using what they've mastered to take risks and reap the benefits. That's what he did on X (the platform formerly known as Twitter). Anybody who knows George knows he's a king of quips and a beast with "yo mama" jokes (and if you don't, let Google show you the light). At the time he joined, he was well into a successful, decade-long run as a headliner in Las Vegas when he got curious about the platform's potential for comedy and decided to play with it to see what would happen. He hadn't joined before, because he didn't want to give his jokes away for free, but he eventually saw it as a way to try out material in 140 characters or less. He started posting and refining his content, while using his marketing expertise to analyze and maximize his impact, turning his account into an instant feedback machine for his jokes that also introduced him to a new audience of just under a million followers. He later turned his success online into print, publishing his 2020 book of his best tweets called *Bulltwit . . . and Whatnot.* The lesson for building power: take your expertise, developed from your core skills and value, from an arena where you know it works, and adapt and apply it to a new one to add to your value and growth.

Like George did with his X/Twitter experiment, many people found power in the pivot during the pandemic. As I said back in chapter 2, many people left their jobs during COVID-19 in search of something better. If the pandemic wasn't your catalyst to adapt, perhaps another life moment caused you to shift your priorities or your career focus. Regardless of when it happened or why, the outcome is the same—we learn there's a lot of elasticity in what we do and the ways that we can do it. Following this philosophy is what keeps us not only employed and employable but engaged in what we're doing. Everyone at some point experiences a certain amount of boredom or a lack of challenge in their work, particularly once they've achieved a sense of mastery. The trick is taking that moment and turning it into something else that expands the territory that you can reach.

If you're early in your career, you may have particular areas of your work that you're most interested in. Those are indicators of where your mastery could come from; where your expertise could be based, where your career path will lead you. What helps you figure out what that is, as I mentioned in chapter 5, is saying yes to everything. It's the advice I always give interns and anyone just starting out in the media business. Say yes to every opportunity until it's a hard no.

That's what worked for me when I started out in radio after college. I didn't care at first what position I had. However, as I tried out each role—copywriter, traffic reporter, news reporter, disc jockey—I discovered I really liked being a jock, an on-air personality. From there, I learned I had a gift for being a cohost, for helping other people shine. I also wanted to work mornings, the biggest shift of the day, so that's what I did, sharing microphones with some of the top names in the industry: Steve Harvey, Tom Joyner, Doug Banks, George Wallace. I took all the information in they had to share as I made my way, focusing on how what I learned on the morning show could apply to my own show down the road.

As your own career progresses, you'll start to say "no" more, a sign that you're finding your expertise and specialty. This is what often happens in the middle of your career: You understand what you could possibly do, an expansion in one very specific category of your job. Sometimes, it plays out a different way, where your yeses take you away from your original goal at first, but all the experiences you get along the way build your power so you can fulfill it.

That's what happened to actor Finesse Mitchell. His career encompasses a wide variety of entertainment media—comedy, performing, TV hosting, podcasting, and writing—but he had his sights set on one more in the comedy world. He always dreamed of owning his own comedy club. He made his first attempt in the mid-2000s when he was fresh off *Saturday Night Live* and on the road doing stand-up. "I got really close," Finesse said. "I had an investor and everything fell through."

Before he got his next shot at the dream, he had some serious lessons to learn that would serve him well later. The first was about his own discipline and motivation. He told me: "My biggest thing that I had to overcome . . . I had to forgive myself for not giving *Saturday Night Live* my all. . . . I didn't do my best. I had to own that. And once I got that out of my head, I stopped living in yesterday."

His dream stayed on hold as the opportunities in acting and comedy kept coming, but he remained true to his dreams, saying, "Comedy ended up taking off . . . but it was like how do I become the business exec and real estate mogul? . . . I got goals."

He reached that goal in 2022 when he became president of Laugh Factory, the number one chain of comedy clubs in the country. Finesse also shared with me that pivoting between so many career interests taught him a crucial lesson in business strategy: "We don't give enough stuff the attention it deserves, because we're all ready to move on to get this other thing going and then we drop the ball on our baby and then we got to come back and pick that up. So, what I've started doing is taking something a little bit further along, really close to the finish line, before I start something else."

That new strategy paid off with regular TV show appearances, movie deals, and content development projects for Laugh Factory performers. He learned that: "You can't give up, you can't leave a course. But when you get a little bit of momentum and traction, you're gonna hit a wall, you're gonna hit a lull, you gotta stay just as excited as when you got the first momentum because it comes in waves."

Some students in my graduate program enrolled because they'd hit a wall. They wanted to lead a team but didn't have the knowledge or experience to get promoted. Even though they were already accomplished in their fields, such as engineering or financial analysis, for them to move forward, they had to become a manager of teams. They needed to expand their skill set, focus on the role they wanted, and learn how to do it better than anyone else. When you get to the end of the mid-career period, you may say to yourself, *I'm going higher, which means going wider.* As you move up in management, you need expertise in a variety of arenas that have little to do with what got you there in the first place.

Wrapping your head around developing new abilities can be challenging, especially in this sense, because it can feel like you're leaving your core expertise behind to embrace something that may not be as true or authentic to you. You can build your power while remaining true to yourself by using that new capacity to expand your impact in your specialty. Who better to lead a team with your expertise than someone who has held that job and shares that experience? Positions with more responsibility often come with more influence. You can use what you know to implement changes you didn't have the power to do before. Become an advocate for your colleagues and develop new ideas that will work. This has happened for my entire career in radio—all of my managers have been on-air at some point in their careers, some continue to be while taking on management roles. Their understanding of our work gives them the insight to help us become better at it. This kind of growth can be an opportunity to once again be curious about what you know and how it could be applied in a new way.

This is a big generalization, but I find that engineers are amazing problem-solvers. That's why so many of them are project managers outside of their area of expertise. What is a project manager but a problem-solver? Same thing goes for computer scientists: People understand that computer scientists are going to be good at organizing information because of the way they formulate programming. Their skills are transferable and often valued even more in a new environment.

The same can be true for all of us. I went to grad school to find out what I knew and how I could apply it elsewhere; to understand what I was taking for granted. Turns out, I took my ten thousand hours in for granted, assuming that everybody knows what I know. But everybody *doesn't* know. So, it becomes a matter of learning how to utilize your skills differently, in a way that serves your authentic self and others.

What skills do you take for granted? How can you utilize them in a new way?

In chapter 4, where we covered *Live It*, it was all about the individual—becoming more aware of ourselves and understanding the importance of how we impact other people and create connection, how our nonverbal behavior affects how what we say is received by others and what we can do to uphold our part of any exchange of communication. Those concepts and processes automatically come into play in your skills discovery process: The whole point, as I said, is to look at yourself and take it all in. To do that in conjunction with your skills, follow these four steps:

- Take inventory first. What are you good at? Refer to my authenticity exercise: think about the work you do, how it benefits others, and why those benefits are important to you.

- Assess all the skills you have and determine the connecting thread.

- Whittle them down into skill sets; the work you do daily or on a regular basis—what are the skills behind that? What do they actually mean? What categories do they fall into?

- Survey every situation through the lens of your expertise.

For example, the students in my strategic media relations class in Northwestern's MSc program had a wide variety of undergraduate degrees. Several math majors took communication classes and realized they had a strong interest in this field but struggled to see how the two could be connected. I explained that many opportunities exist within media to use their computative and analytic skills, including synthesizing data to target specific products to certain demographics or to help their understanding of the ways data can inform how they tell a story.

USE YOUR WORDS

Not everyone is going to understand why you make the choices you do. Partners, friends, bosses, or parents (at any age) can be difficult to convince that you're on the right path for you. For several students in my class, it was a tough talk, explaining why they wanted a career in media or communications instead of medicine or law. The disappointment was palpable. Belinda Chang, an award-winning sommelier, writer, and Chicago restaurateur, had that experience with her parents to an extreme. They didn't speak with her for a year after she told them she wanted to focus on fine dining in the food and beverage industry. Belinda's advice for my class (which applies to anyone, really) about handling difficult conversations like these is, "You have to tell the story of what this actually means to you and what impact it's going to have."

As you explore the different ways you can utilize your existing skills, it might lead to a change in your priorities or a major career shift. If you are a mathematician who wants to jump into the media industry, or a writer who wants to trade journalism for grant writing, other people might be confused, or even taken aback, by this change. It's crucial that you are able to tell the story of why this shift is bringing you closer to your authentic self. You need to deftly explain how you went from point A to point B, especially if they're not industry-related.

Bela Gandhi is well-practiced at telling her story, because it's a fascinating and successful one. It ranges from her running part of her family's Fortune 100 manufacturing business to becoming known as "the fairy godmother of love." Quite an evolution of discovery! She founded her Smart Dating Academy more than fifteen years ago, leaving her corporate life behind.

"Whatever you do, whatever you study, whatever you first come out doing doesn't have to define you," she said. "It's not your end-all, be-all. If you know what your gift is, and you're brave enough and fearlessly authentic enough to do it, you can get there, too."

Bela didn't see her gift as a career option at first and had no idea what she wanted to do with her life. "I would envy my friends that would be like, 'I've known since I was five years old that I wanted to be a journalist.' 'I've known since I was eight years old that I wanted to be an ER doctor.' I was like, 'I changed my major four times last week.' I was totally that kid. I'm the child of first-generation Indian immigrants. If y'all know anything about our culture, we produce professionals . . . I didn't fit in anywhere into these rubrics."

She ended up going to business school, the least offensive option, according to her, earning degrees in finance and German. She worked as a management consultant at Arthur Andersen right out of school and realized pretty quickly she was in the wrong place.

"I was like a flower that had been put in a dark vacuum. I was wilted, sad, and for a year, I kind of figured my way around how to survive there. That's when my dad was like, 'Yeah, you're bored. Why don't you maybe think about utilizing that useless German degree that I paid for? Why don't you take our Teflon business . . . to Europe?' I thought, *I don't know a damn thing about chemistry*. But he said something to me that changed the course of my life. We were on our patio deck . . . I said to him, 'Dad, I took one class of chemistry in high school.' My dad's a chemical engineer, and I was not good at it. 'What can I do for you? Yeah, I speak German but then what?' He looked at me and he's like, 'You are only limited to your own ambition. Don't ask me that question again.' And he turned around and walked off the deck."

Though she couldn't wrap her head around his admonition right away, she eventually understood what he was telling her: you can do whatever you want—that's your only limit. Consequently, she resigned from Arthur Andersen seven days later and joined the family business. It wasn't an easy transition, though. As the owner's daughter, she felt immediate pressure to succeed.

"If you start a job anywhere else, you start at zero, right? People are willing to talk to you. They're like, okay, let's see who you are. When you start out with the same last name as the owner, you start out at negative one hundred. And when you're female, negative two hundred. They're like, 'Oh, here's the princess. Let's see what she's going to do.' I was the first one there in the morning; I turned the lights on. I was the last one there; I turned the lights out—for years. It took that long for them to go, 'All right, we respect you.'"

She credits that experience, however, for her ability to transition from corporate life to starting her own company.

"It was everything. . . . If I had taken the safe route, like I'm going to stay at Arthur Andersen and I'm going to work thirteen years; I'm going to be partner . . . I knew that I had to go. If I had not experienced the role of climbing from negative two hundred to zero, driving forklifts, all those survival skills ultimately . . . it built super strong skills at a very young age. I was thrust into leadership at twenty-three, traveling to five continents a year. I was 100 percent responsible for my U-turn into entrepreneurship because I don't know any differently."

Those skills Bela learned working for the family business would help her succeed as an entrepreneur later, but it took time for her to put it together with her matchmaking prowess. She discovered she had a knack for it after she got to college. Her first match was her roommate with a guy she met in the dorms her freshman year. "I was like, 'You're gonna marry my roommate.' It took me two years to get them to go on a date. But when they did, I'll tell you what, they were engaged two years later, and they've now been married for twenty-three years." Hundreds of matches later, her clients say, "It's like going to Harvard Business School but for dating and relationships."

By following all the bread crumbs from the varied experiences along her path, Bela found her purpose.

So, how can you do the same? Whether you're just starting your career or in the middle of it, it's about constantly taking stock of the first question in my authenticity exercise: What work do you do? Then connecting an emotional component to it. Ask yourself what you enjoy doing. Or, just as important, what you dread doing. We all have stuff we don't like about our jobs, but when you know all the tasks you dread, the more easily you can see what's left—the good stuff. And that's what you use to create something new for yourself. If that's not entirely possible, then find a position that includes more of the functions that you love and less of the ones you hate, and accept there's always going to be a mix. For most people just starting out, the ratio of work tasks you love versus those you hate is pretty lopsided. But as you move through your career, you can use more skills that you prize and shift to strengths that better serve your purpose and that you prefer.

Bela left the family business after the company was bought by a multinational firm that had big plans for her, including a promotion and a move to a new city. She turned it down—she had a two-year-old and a house. This was her opportunity to start her own dating service, but it still took her a while to have the courage to make the leap.

Those management and entrepreneurial skills she picked up from working in her family business would come in handy soon enough, but first her matchmaking skills were put to good use when they found their way into her work, as clients would ask for recommendations on using overseas manufacturers. She said: "I'm just matchmaking all the while. . . . It's this process that you can deploy in any aspect of your life . . . I would get to know the personality of the factories in Asia—I was there five times a year. And I'm like, you know what, I think this is a good factory for you, and then start to match our corporate clients with vendors in Asia."

The longer she did that, the more it became evident that it was time to commit to using her gift and move on to become the matchmaker and dating coach she was meant to be. The transition wasn't easy, however, or free from doubts. "I went through some dark, sad, depressed times, until I knew I wanted to do this dating thing. But it was fear. It was fear of failure. It was fear of, I had this big career, what are people gonna say? . . . Worrying about what I thought other people would think if it didn't go well."

Then one day she stumbled across Marc Grabowski's article on "Failure versus Regret," and it compelled her to experience the feelings now that she might have later if she gave into that fear of failure and didn't do anything with her dating business. So, she did an exercise where she envisioned telling her future grandchildren the story of her dating business, as if she had started it and failed. It wasn't a pleasant task for her to imagine her dream business failing before she had even gotten it started, especially since she was sharing that failure with these future family members she eventually wanted to inspire. But when she envisioned the regret scenario—imagining telling those same hopeful young hearts that she had this dream but didn't do anything to make it come true and never gave her business a chance at all—she experienced what it might be like to live with that feeling fifty years down the line. It was far, far worse.

Going through that exercise convinced her that she never wanted to say, "I wish I would have done that." And she decided that day she would do it—no more caring what other people thought, no explanations or delays. A month later, she was in business. Her advice now? "Focus on failure versus regret. Play the long game in your mind, people." Daring, but wise.

If you're thinking of shifting careers but don't see how your specific experience might apply elsewhere, I can iden-tify with that. It's so hard to see other applications when your specialty feels unique. Instead of focusing on what you think you can't do, focus first on your qualities and the soft skills you've developed as pathways to building your power. I had to do that, because I thought broadcast had little synergy with other industries. But every time I go into a room now, I'm hit with—and relieved by—the reality that my experience does apply there. One client I consult for is always storytelling, trying to persuade someone that their product is beneficial. It boils down to the same thing I experienced on TV and radio: How are you going to say something so somebody hears you? This process, of course, also includes figuring out who needs what you have to offer, the *Sell It* piece; knowing your value and what the benefit is. But when you start to see how any of your skills apply elsewhere, you've opened the door to finding more of those opportunities.

I'm sure author Ashlee Piper had to go through a similar process when she moved from political strategist to sustainability expert. On the surface, the two couldn't seem more different, but the communication skills she needed in her first career certainly apply to her second one.

Her growing interest in ecological preservation and animal rescue is what compelled her to make the leap. People have come to view her book *Give a Sh*t: Do Good. Live Better. Save the Planet* as the sustainability bible, doling out advice in a way that is accessible and focused on using our personal power to impact the environment.

"I didn't find really a lot of guidance out there that resonated with me. I did find a lot of people who were doing incredibly ambitious and interesting things in the world of personal sustainability. They were making their own clothes and milling their own flour . . . stuff I thought was really cool. But it wasn't necessarily feasible for my lifestyle. On the flip side, there were all sorts of books out there that existed around climate change . . . but they were incredibly cerebral. I really wanted to start to talk about sustainability and the offshoots of it, like minimalism and green beauty and vegan fashion, all those things that are more intertwined in more mainstream media."

So, Ashlee decided to teach us how to save the world, her way.

"One of the biggest things I want to help people reconnect with is their personal power," she told me. "How powerful our personal choices and habits are, and how easy it is to simply shift a few of those, and actually make a big, big difference in what is a very large, very scary, very real problem that requires all hands on deck."

She got her first mainstream media exposure on our morning show, joining us for regular TV segments. "I found it so enjoyable because you wanted to present it in a fun way . . . we made it not seem crunchy and weird and uncomfortable. That was always the hurdle for me is how can I make the messaging something that's going to be resonant with people and not make them think those things that are stigmas around sustainability: it's crunchy, it's expensive, it's socially isolating, it's weird and fringy, it doesn't make a difference."

When I asked Ashlee if what she's doing now is what she was meant to do, if this has been a process of discovery of the things she really loves, she was confident in her response.

"It's been really throwing things against the wall, so to speak, that I'd never done before and kind of going with that and seeing if it works. I'll be totally transparent: I'm not in a place yet where I'd like to be with this work . . . but I look at where I was ten years ago, and you kind of have to look at the growth, but I do feel really strongly that sustainability is a place and purpose for me."

Ashlee's commitment to herself, her authenticity, and following her passions is a testament to how you find your purpose and build power through it—and it's the reason her message resonates with her audience so strongly.

"When I left political strategy, I had zero idea of what I was going to do. I thought I was going to maybe go lobby . . . and when I explored that, I was like, *Oh, I can't support myself on that.* I sort of lived and still sometimes live in this space of 'I'll have a different career that's my keep-the-lights-on job.' But I still nurture this on the side, because I can't give it up . . . it's just constantly something I feel like I want to do and have ideas around . . . I've had many chapters or seasons in my life, and I will continue to because we're never kind of done. We're never fully fleshed out, developed people until we're absorbed back into the universe or whatever happens to us . . . I just don't feel that afraid to try things . . . there's not much I think I can't do. It's just a matter of determining, with a limited amount of time and energy, what do I want to do?"

For Mignon Francois, it was about what she must do. Her story is proof of building power through authenticity—both in yourself and by encouraging it in others. Mignon was a busy mom with some big problems when she doubled down on her belief in herself and her ability to meet any challenge. She created what would become the Cupcake Collection more than fifteen years ago with her last five dollars and no prior baking experience or business knowledge. At the time, her family was struggling, and she did the only thing she could think of to survive—holding a bake sale to raise much-needed funds. She turned that initial investment into a cupcake empire, with stores in two states and nationwide delivery.

What's even more important to Mignon is the history behind her company. Her family was born and raised on the Louisiana sugar plantation that now supplies her business; they harvested the sugarcane.

"I am making a living, sending people to college, making a name for our family, passing it on for generations. . . . Here I am showing up on the scene . . . in the same industry where my grandmothers could not have free enterprise, but it was their labor that caused someone else to be able to gain wealth. It's the thing I'm teaching my team who's with me now, that you are in the business of your labor. It's allowing me to teach them something that they can harness as well as develop, so they know that you don't work for me, you work *with* me . . . I'm coming to you not as a boss, but as a client, looking for labor that I can purchase so that I could get my product to market."

Mignon's reframing of how we view work resonates so strongly for me. Some people do feel like they're enslaved to their work or to their employers, because without that job, what do they have and what will they do? But if you can reimagine your labor as something you own—whether you're working for yourself or someone else—you're back in the driver's seat. You get to decide who you're lending it to and for how much. That price obviously changes as you grow in your career. You're not worth as much money if you're inexperienced or right out of college since you're still learning, and part of your pay is what you learn on the job. As you gain expertise and start to tell the story of how you got it, that's how people understand the value of it. But the shift happens internally long before you get to that point. The moment you decide you own your work, you can see the value you have and the potential in the value you're growing through your work and education. It becomes a source to build your authentic power and confidence in a way that's hard to shake.

"We're talking about a father who was born on the plantation, and his daughters who are working in the industry," she said, "and we get to be in charge. We get to have true freedom. That's what I love about entrepreneurship—I get to own my own labor. I get to say what I do with my labor. That's what I teach my team all the time . . . you tell me how we're going to handle this. I don't want to be the smartest person in the room . . . I need you to bring the ideas and the concepts and the processes. . . . We need all these people who are going to bring their gifts and talents and experiences to the table."

Mignon's work philosophy is a model for how, when we value all the things we know and really understand what we bring to the table, we will organically and authentically build our power. Those skills and knowledge will change but you need to recognize how your work, your value, and your authenticity impact your career over time. Having a sense of discovery is key to identifying your many different abilities—not just your core job duties, but the soft skills and qualities it often takes to propel you to the next level.

Now it's time to find your own power in building a bridge between your current skills and a new opportunity while mastering your fears of change. Your commitment to yourself, your commitment to exploring what's next on your journey of discovery, should never end. You get to make it what you want it to be: a more authentic expression of yourself so you can stand out among others, understanding how nobody can outdo you being you.

BE FREE AND BE YOU
AUTHENTICITY ACTION

A thought exercise for you: Take an inventory of your life and find what excites you and gives you purpose. Think about exploring new opportunities. It's not about starting over, rather evolving and seeing a connection between what you're doing now and another situation you'd want to be in where you can be free to share more of you with your audience.

CHAPTER 8

Insider Media Secrets

BROADCASTING YOUR BEST SELF

The biggest test of your Fearless Authenticity is how well you can tell the story about your value. I hope, at this point, you've gotten some practice in and gotten better at doing that one-on-one or in small groups. Now it's time to trust the confidence and self-awareness you've built up to 1) present yourself in your best way through *Live It*, 2) trust your ability to weave a compelling tale in *Tell It*, and 3) use your knowledge on how to appeal to your audience by serving their needs through *Sell It*. Then put it all together, kick it up a notch, and deliver your stories about yourself and your value to as many people as possible. In other words, *Be Brave* because the camera is on and you're standing in front of it. Ready to go in 3 . . . 2 . . . 1!

You may not have a specific goal to appear on television, in movies, or even in a podcast, but you will need to broadcast your best self and your value at some point. We are all content creators, whether or not we are aware of it—or admit it. You already know at this point in your Fearless Authenticity journey that just doing your work well isn't a guarantee that it will be seen and recognized; we have to tell that story ourselves. This is the next step in that process and one that's common in business—scaling up that effort to expand reach and make an impact. We all have access to several social media platforms to accomplish that, and between those and virtual work and events, we've all done something that's pretty close to traditional broadcasting already. It's time to do it right.

Most of us think of media as news programs or talk shows, but the word *media* literally means "middle," and can be any method of communication *in the middle* of two points. So, every time you find yourself inside a box on a screen meeting virtually, recording a voice memo or Loom to leave notes for or explain something to someone you work with, or post a video for your family and friends on social media, you are technically a media personality. You dive even deeper into that role when you start sharing your thoughts with the intention of building an audience on social media, for a podcast, or to pursue a position as an expert guest on traditional media (television or radio). Wherever we are on that range, it's essential to perform and communicate our messages well—which I define as connecting with our intended audience with confidence and composure, and maybe even with a little extra razzle-dazzle pixie dust sprinkled on top. Think of this as the natural progression to build up the three Foundations for Success, especially *Live It* and *Tell It*—you're already being more intentional in your Fearless Authenticity and telling those stories in the settings you know; now we'll add more dimension to them, exploring how to *Be You* and tell them in different ways, in different places. Growth happens when you stretch beyond what you know, testing the limits of what you've already tried out.

To do that successfully, we first have to take ownership of our communications. Too often, we take what we say for granted. We think communication doesn't have a purpose if we're not making money from it. Then why do we take the time and effort to share selfies or make a funny TikTok video for friends? If something is important enough to us to say at all, we should prepare to say it well. We can most easily fall into the trap of skipping preparation when we're comfortable with our subject matter and assume our next experience will be like the last. I've even done it. I had to do a presentation for one of my classes in grad school and wrote it out, but didn't practice because I just knew I would do well—I mean, that's what I do for a living, right? Wrong. I got up there and stumbled through my presentation because I wasn't organized, then got embarrassed and nervous when I wasn't prepared for the thoughtful and challenging questions my classmates asked me. It was a new situation with new material, but I assumed my experience would carry me through and it just wasn't enough. And I can't tell you how many times I've had someone I'm training say to me, "I just do better when I wing it," only to come back to me for help after they did the same thing I did for my class and the same thing happened to them. When you know it's important but you don't treat it like it is, you're flirting with failure. And that may be the only chance you get.

I believe everything we express has more impact and power when we apply the same sort of rigor and intention to it that we use for our most important communications. And here's the thing: As we move forward, the way we share information is only going to become more important and enduring. It will live forever online. Everything we post becomes part of our body of work, searchable by generations to come—forever. There will always be a record of what we've said and how we've said it. So, the question becomes, what are we actually putting out there for the rest of time? Is it a faithful representation of who we truly are? Are we sharing the thoughts, ideas, and wisdom we were born to share? If we have messages we think are worth hearing, we need to put a little effort into making sure they're heard the way we intend. Because the more effort we put into those important moments, the easier it is to tap into that mindset during the casual ones. We become more present and accountable every time we engage on all the platforms available to us. That way, we're more likely to leave something useful and impactful behind that reflects our legacy. So, how do you do that, as your most true, authentic self?

Be prepared. Simple, yes, but as we all know, simple isn't easy. I've got plenty of stories to tell you about guests on my radio and television shows who've tried to wing it (like my clients), only to crash and burn. This chapter is designed to share my expertise and give you a proven process for preparing for any kind of communication, performance, or appearance, whether it's a work presentation, Zoom call, speaking engagement, media interview, podcast, or TikTok video. You'll learn how to be your fearless, authentic self through practice; how to rehearse; how to prepare yourself; how to avoid wardrobe and makeup missteps; how to anticipate situations; how to engage with your audience; and how to have confidence on camera.

The most important piece to remember, the number one thing you need to know to be successful as a content creator is this: the medium you're using is never your audience! It's not the camera, the platform's algorithm, or the stage you're on. Those are just tools you use to reach and serve your audience. Know your audience first, and then use those tools to talk to them.

No matter your medium of expression, preparation is the key to preventing stress, embarrassment, missed opportunities, or going viral for all the wrong reasons. When you host a live television show, you get used to guests who are a little nervous, especially if it's their first time on TV. Nervousness is a natural reaction to a new setting: studios with all the lights and cameras and all the people running around can be intimidating. It becomes part of your job as host to calm people down in situations like that. And when a guest has to do a demonstration—such as chefs, bakers, or animal trainers (one brought a python that ended up in my shirt!)—that only turns up the intensity!

Nothing beat the time a bartender came on the show to make a couple special drinks for the holidays. I knew he was nervous, but before we went on, we got him laughing and he seemed like he was going to be okay. By the time we got through the short introduction to his segment, all that had changed. I looked over to welcome him to the show and he was white as a sheet, with huge beads of sweat on his brow and upper lip (always a dead giveaway that things aren't going well internally). I knew he was in trouble. But he surprised us by getting through the introduction and our opening chitchat perfectly fine. So, we relaxed a bit because, usually, if someone starts off well, they end well. But we should've stopped while we were ahead on this one. When we asked him to make his first drink, this poor guy's hands were shaking so badly that the first shot of liquor he tried to measure into a glass went everywhere, including on me! I grabbed his arm to try and steady his hand for the close-up, which didn't work so well because he kept trying to do it right. By the end of the segment, so much booze had spilled on the counter—and us—that we smelled like a distillery. And you know I hate to see good booze go to waste. When I tell you that poor man wanted to crawl out of the studio when it was all said and done, that's an understatement. Afterward, he admitted that he hadn't actually practiced making the cocktails for the segment and had been out late drinking the night before because he was so nervous about being on with us. Well, that strategy *never* works—for anything! So, let's give you one that does.

Whether you're doing an in-person presentation, Zoom call, media interview, podcast, or YouTube video, create a process to prepare for it. The process is what grounds us, gives us comfort and confidence, and, ultimately, keeps us calm and focused in the moment. Whether or not you're aware of it, you approach every day with a process to get yourself ready for all the things you need to do—this is no different. You're doing something that's new to your everyday routine, so having a new process to help you get ready for it will help you do your best—especially if it's something that kicks your nerves into overdrive, like appearing on camera. Then, as time goes on, it will become part of you—the process you rely on to be consistent and always perform your best.

Let's start with the meat of it: your content. This is where my Foundations for Success (*Live It, Tell It, Sell It* from chapters 4, 5, and 6) will serve and benefit you. Here's how to use that approach and apply it in these situations.

Whenever you create content, think about your message and what you want your audience to know and take away from it. Please use my Foundations for Success—*Live It, Tell It, Sell It*—in the order that works best for you and your situation; I often recommend that you start with *Sell It* first.

Ask yourself a few questions about who you're talking to and really get to know them. Next, ask the big questions: *Why do/should they care? How can I serve them by addressing that?* Then use those answers to tailor what you want to share with them to align with who they are and what they care about in the manner they prefer. It's important to have a grasp of the facts and a concise, well-delivered message, but successful communication is also about understanding your purpose for sharing that message so it connects in a way that's relevant and useful for your audience and resonates with them—whether in person or through a camera, live on Instagram, or in a video on YouTube.

Here's one way I do this part: When I record my "Self-Care Sunday" videos for social media, I focus the content on a challenge I've overcome or I'm working on that has taught me a valuable lesson. They all come from the realization that, no matter how stupid I feel about something that's challenging me, I'm not the first one to have felt it, and I definitely won't be the last. Knowing my followers respond to those kinds of breakthrough realizations, I share my frustrations and the next steps I'm taking in the hope that somebody else may benefit from hearing me talk about them. So, while "Self-Care Sunday" is for me—acknowledging and recording where I am and what I've learned at this point—it's also what my *Sell It* analysis has told me can help my followers gain some insight into their own challenges and feel less alone.

Once you've got *Sell It* covered, move on to *Tell It.* You know your audience, now break down your message for them into key talking points: the information you want them to take from your content. As I discussed in chapter 5, this information is best conveyed by making it stick in their memory and hearts through storytelling. Sharing a story that elicits an emotion in them will be the best way to make it memorable.

Now, we're into *Live It.* There are two factors to consider:

1. The manner in which you deliver your content
2. The environment in which the content will be delivered

Here, I want you to reflect on how to incorporate the concepts we've talked about into the design of how you'll deliver your message. Next, we'll outline how to turn this into a process for you to do, step-by-step.

Consider what you learned about yourself in chapter 4: how you use your nonverbal behaviors to support your message, where you get tripped up, what will make your story come alive, and how your tone, facial expressions, gestures, and everything you do affect the people you talk to. Incorporate all that you've learned about yourself into your storytelling so it has the effect and/or elicits the action you want from your audience.

Consider what the setting or environment will look like and how you'll tell your message in it. Ask yourself where it is and what that situation calls for. Is it at work or another corporate setting—in a conference room, behind a podium, or on a Zoom call? Maybe you're doing a demonstration or interview at your local TV station, and you'll be on set with the anchors. Or perhaps you're making a tutorial for your YouTube channel, where you'll be on your DIY set with your props and tools. Wherever you'll be, make sure your message is organized in a way that matches that particular setting.

Going back to my earlier example of my "Self-Care Sunday" videos, here's how *Tell It* and *Live It* come into play together. For *Tell It*, I want what I share to be easy to take in, so it has to be relatively short and relaxed. I distill my experience down to its essence and truth, because that's what I think my followers are really looking for and it's also what I want them to remember. It's not about telling the whole story here, only the part that's relevant to my audience: the lesson I've learned from going through the situation.

And to layer on *Live It*, I focus on telling it in a way that makes it memorable for them—in this case, the emotion it evokes. I always shoot these when I'm in bed because I want it to feel intimate, open, and transparent. To me, that's the best setting to share what I've learned in a way that will hopefully model that same behavior and vibe for them. The informal setting allows my followers to lower their guard enough to really hear what I'm saying and feel the emotions that could help them on their journey—less alone, more aware, braver, or excited to try something new.

I use these videos on LinkedIn because their casual nature makes them stand out among the professional posts there, but many of my other posts on that channel are directly related to challenges at work. I don't use those work-related videos elsewhere, because I wouldn't get much response on platforms that are more topical or personal. Analyze your audience with the strategy and approach you learned in *Sell It* and let that guide how you structure your message—the new variable here is considering and adjusting the setting to impact how your audience receives the message.

Let's move on to the next part of building your preparation process: executing the plan you just made for your message. Rehearse. Practice. Run through. Train. Drill. Pick a word, any word. Whatever you call it, if the outcome and results of delivering your message mean anything to you, do it *for you* before you do it *for real*. As you practice, consider all the components that will feed into your performance.

ANTICIPATE YOUR SPEAKING ENVIRONMENT

Where will you be speaking or recording your content? Try to re-create the setting as closely as possible. Envision yourself in the physical environment and what it will look like or what might be there. Look at every aspect of the setting and how it will affect you: Indoors or outdoors? Small space or huge room? Noise level, audience size, virtual platform, background options, and even weather conditions—all of these elements, big or small, can impact your performance, so do not discount the importance of this step. This is especially important if you get nervous in new situations. Often, nervousness comes from the unfamiliar, and comfort comes from familiarity. The beautiful thing about our brains is that we don't have to physically go somewhere to become familiar with it. If we can imagine it close to how it will really be, it becomes familiar enough, so we'll be less nervous when we get to the real place, even if we've never been there before.

If being on-camera is part of the setting, know that the camera doesn't lie (see "Camera Confidence" below). It's even more important to believe in your message and in yourself. For the people watching to have confidence in what you're saying, you need to have confidence in what you're saying first. For better or worse, people are more likely to give their attention to those who seem worthy of it. If you're not sure of yourself, then they can't be either. Cameras only make this more apparent. So, keep your body language open, your expressions light, and your hand gestures natural and necessary and away from your face.

CAMERA CONFIDENCE

Cameras don't lie. They do, however, have a way of magnifying things—space, physicality, truth, or falsehood. So, unless you're a good actor, don't try to fake it or be who you think you should or are expected to be. Instead, increase your self-awareness.

Cameras often exaggerate movements and features—drawing attention to the very things you don't want the audience to notice. Cameras also absorb an enormous amount of energy. You need just the right amount to come across well and keep your audience's attention.

Too little, and you put people to sleep. Too much, and you look ridiculous.

Case in point: Tom Cruise on *Oprah* when he declared his love for Katie Holmes. He was jumping up and down on the couch like a wild man, stunning the in-studio audience, viewers at home, and even Oprah herself. Anybody who saw it remembers it (not in a good way) and that happened in 2005. Google it, and recall what I said about how what you say and do lives forever on the internet when you see it on a list of his five craziest moments.

Never underestimate the power of the camera.

KNOW THE CONTENT AND WHERE YOU FIT

If you're going to be a guest on a TV show, radio program, podcast, or YouTube live stream, watch or listen to the show content and know what the hosts are usually interested in and how they ask questions. Often, if you're appearing on a show, a producer will get you ready, but familiarity helps immensely. Remember, they're "lending" you their audience and giving you access to them, so your content should serve both your hosts and their audience.

Understand what you're walking into and what could happen, and then prepare for that. For instance, will you be asked questions? If you're on as an expert or newsmaker, then that would be a big yes. Think about what those questions might be and prepare your answers. You may receive possible questions from the program's producer ahead of your appearance, but those are just suggested. The hosts may come up with their own and surprise you. Be sure to consider a wide range of questions and then rehearse your answers, as though you're speaking directly to the host or interviewer.

RECORD, REVIEW, REFINE

I told you in chapter 4 that you might get tired of hearing me say *rehearse, rehearse, rehearse!* How you rehearse is as important as rehearsing itself. Here's how to apply that practice to this situation (and refer to chapter 4 for a deeper dive if you need it):

Record yourself delivering your presentation or your practice interview. Say it out loud, do it in the position you'll be in—standing at your demo area, sitting on a couch or at a desk with hosts on a TV show, or as in my "Self-Care Sunday" videos, lying in bed, being totally relaxed to create that vibe. Your practice session should include your prepared remarks and answers to anticipated questions, if any.

Review the video. Watch it as if you were a member of your audience, and ask yourself if anything you did was distracting and if, overall, you communicated what you'd intended *from the audience's perspective.* If not, find ways to *refine* those moments to get your delivery closer to your intention, whether it's something you can practice or something you'll do in the moment.

When I hosted morning TV, our guests ranged from celebrities to newsmakers, chefs, doctors, authors, and even comedians who were obsessed with feet and tried to lick our toes! I had to be prepared for just about anything to happen because it usually did. One time, we did a segment about a reptile show in town and an animal trainer brought a python into the studio. He asked if I'd like to hold it and I said, "Sure, why not?" One of my friend's brothers had a boa constrictor and I'd been in segments with snakes before, so I wasn't afraid.

He started the segment by introducing me to the reptiles he'd brought. He put the python—we'll call him Petey—around my neck, and as we talked about the event details and other animals, ole Petey proceeded to slither into my shirt and down my sleeve. I knew Petey meant me no harm—he was just trying to stay warm in a cold studio. But as he ventured farther down my sleeve, with his tail down the neck of my blouse, I did start to wonder how we'd get Petey out of his warm spot without ruining my blouse and exposing way more of me than I wanted to. Everybody's reactions as this played out was what made it fun and funny—it was good TV. It all worked out, because we had prepared: before the segment even started, we had talked over what could happen with the trainer and set parameters so that neither Petey nor I was ever in danger. That preparation gave me the confidence to just go with it in the moment.

ON-CAMERA CONSIDERATIONS: BROADCAST MEDIA

While you may be comfortable being on camera for a TikTok video or Zoom call, I have some specific tips for addressing the camera in broadcast media situations or, as most guests would ask the minute they hit the set, where should I look?

- The camera is usually watching you—but you are not usually watching it.

- If you're doing a demonstration, the cameras will follow the action. You don't need to hold up things for the camera or talk to the camera person.

- As a guest in the studio, you will almost never look at the camera.

- The main exception to that rule is if you're on Zoom for a live or taped interview, in which case, you will look directly at the camera.

- If you're at a press conference or delivering a speech to an in-person audience, address the audience. If you look at the camera, it will be okay.

- If you're at a talk show with a live studio audience, focus mainly on the host, but it is okay if you also address the audience. The camera should be the last thing on your mind unless you're the host.

- If you're being interviewed with another person or in a group of people, look at the person who is talking. Remember that you're part of a conversation.

- Overall, the best guests address the hosts or reporters only. They're present for the conversation, not searching for the camera. There's an unspoken rule that only the hosts and reporters communicate directly with their audience, not the guests. That rule can be broken by those highly skilled at engaging the audience, but it's all about knowing what you can get away with.

Your confidence starts with how ready you are to perform at the highest level. Your content is ready and you've rehearsed your performance, but what about your mindset?

Is your head in the right place for whatever content you're sharing? How can you be your most comfortable, authentic self in front of an audience? Maybe your day needs to start with breakfast, a cup of tea, or walking your dog to settle yourself. Don't do anything new that could throw you off or put you into a tailspin. This includes new clothes, shoes, food, drinks, or technology.

WARDROBE DOS AND DON'TS

- Wear colors that look good on you and you feel good in.

- Jewel tones and bold solid colors complement most people.

- All black can be boring, and it really doesn't hide anything.

- All-white can be problematic, because it can be glaringly bright, especially on darker skin tones.

- Look the part: dress as you would to go to work or what people in your profession are expected to look like.

- Be careful with patterns. Some small patterns, especially those with fine lines, can look like moiré (an irregular wavy or ripple pattern) on camera and big patterns can be distracting. It's not a hard and fast rule—just a guideline.

You want people to pay the most attention to you and your message, not what you're wearing (unless you're a model, stylist, or designer, then that's the whole point, isn't it?).

MAKEUP MODE

- Wear what you usually do to feel comfortable.

- Do not try anything out for the first time. Stick to what you know looks good on your face. (Oh, the horror stories I can tell about false eyelashes alone: falling off during segments to the point I had to snatch them off a guest's face, or being so long that a guest couldn't wear her eyeglasses and spent the whole segment looking everywhere instead of at me.)

• Blot or powder your face/forehead to reduce shine, especially if you sweat, have oily skin, or are bald.

Whatever you do, make sure it enhances how you look and feel, instead of distracting the audience or drawing their attention away from you or your message.

As you prep for any kind of situation, remember, your overall goal is to be your authentic self in what could be an unnatural and unfamiliar setting. To help with your process, if you have a routine for your workday, create something similar for your content creator days. They may be less frequent, but these tasks are just as important, so incorporate them into your job.

The best content creators are comfortable in whatever setting they're in and consistently deliver quality content— reliable information that's well communicated, engaging, and interesting.

Many people try to reinvent the wheel every time they do something new. That's unnecessary. When you know what brings you comfort, you can leverage those practices to help you execute what you need to do. By giving yourself comfort, you give yourself what you need to succeed. This may not seem like much, but it is a struggle I often see with my clients.

Case in point: Andrea wanted to expand her mental health practice and her presence in the industry by creating online videos. But she was extremely self-conscious of her appearance and voice and was afraid she would say something wrong or not get the response she wanted. These fears led her to script everything, but she could never get through a recording session and gave up, never posting anything.

I worked with her to develop a much simpler process that would make her more comfortable and remove the obstacles she had set up for herself. Instead of following a script that made her feel like she needed to be perfect, she used more of an outline and just talked about what she already knew, using stories to help illustrate her point. She also changed the taping location to her office, where she already felt at ease talking to clients. The biggest change of all was that she reviewed the recording, something she had never done before.

This new process helped her recognize that she had been overthinking everything. She realized this format was more natural to her; it was the way she related to her current clients, and she knew it worked because of their previous positive feedback. She now had the courage to put the content she created out into the world. She posted her first video right after we recorded and reviewed it. She continued to post new videos several times a week and built an online audience immediately.

Andrea learned that when you give yourself a way to see what you say the way others do, you can understand what to do better, build your confidence, and give yourself the freedom to say what you have to say, reach the audiences you want, and achieve your goals. This goes for any kind of content creator. Consistently creating quality content is the best way to build your following on social media (no matter the platform or algorithm) and get invited back as a guest on a show or as a speaker at a conference. When you spend the energy to craft your message carefully, prepare your delivery, and fuel it with your *Fearless Authenticity*, you serve your audience and make the connections you need to be successful.

BE BRAVE, BE FREE, BE YOU AUTHENTICITY ACTION

Determine why you want to share something with your audience. Get clear on how it moves your purpose forward. Most important, understand what is in it for your audience and how you can make a connection.

Then *Live It, Tell It, Sell It*.

CHAPTER 9

Everyday Relationships with Authenticity

I've found through the process of refining my work and writing this book that the greatest areas for growth on my *Fearless Authenticity* journey have been in my personal relationships. I've made my share of mistakes in relationships with friends, family members, and especially significant others. Where I am now is much better than where I've been, and a big part of that is practicing what I preach and using my Foundations for Success (*Live It, Tell It, Sell It*—see chapters 4, 5, and 6) to transform my everyday life.

Even though this chapter is about improving relationships through *Fearless Authenticity*, I don't think of this as relationship advice. I only want to offer my perspective as someone who has seen how this process can make things better, after participating in flawed relationships of all kinds and witnessing the demise of many marriages and unions as the "single friend." (Yes, if you didn't know, that is a thing.

Most people find it easier to vent about a divorce or breakup to a single friend because there's less risk involved—of being judged, excluded from a coupled-up friend group, or just plain old fear that their bad relationship juju is contagious. And I've found this to be true across genders and orientations—when your relationship is failing, your single friends know far more about it than the couples in your circle.)

There are as many iterations and permutations of how things fall apart as there are people on this earth. When you sit back and look at it all, you start to see the patterns. From where I sit, it almost always comes down to two things:

1. Not dealing with your own issues and expecting your partner, friend, colleague, or family member to make up for past damage or fix your issues for you
2. Communication (the core of any successful relationship)

Now, what I will say about number one is that I absolutely believe we and the people in our lives (partners, friends, family, colleagues) can help one another in our growth, healing, and path to living well. But healing is an inside job that nobody can do for you. And try as you might, you cannot hide your issues in your relationships, especially the intimate ones. Some would say that's the whole point of relationships—to see ourselves and all the things we're dealing with more fully. Whether you're always trying to fix your friends, twisting yourself into pretzels to live up to your manager's or family's expectations, or using your partner as an emotional scratching post to make the pain go away, whatever it is, the lesson you're here to learn will repeat itself until you heal and break that cycle. And if you're having trouble doing that, therapy may be in your best interest (I know it's helped me immensely, but do what works for you).

As for number two, on the surface, it sounds completely reasonable to say, "If I've got to explain everything to you, I may as well do it myself." We all want to be understood, heard, and seen, preferably by osmosis, not by explanation. Nobody wants to have to explain themselves all the time. And the romantic fantasies and fairy tales that we've grown up with tell us the person who loves us will just know how to make us happy. First off, it's not up to the people we love (no matter how we define the relationship) to make us happy. Just like healing, that's an inside job. It is literally impossible to bestow happiness upon another human being. Second, you do have to communicate and, yes, you'll need to explain some necessary information to make all your relationships work and thrive.

Let's start with relationship roles and how that plays into this. Of course, the first one that comes to mind is the one we have with our parents. We spend most of our lives seeing them as Mama and Daddy and less as real people. Then there's a point, usually in early adulthood, where we realize they are whole human beings with many sides beyond the roles they fill in our lives. I remember very distinctly the moment I saw my mother as Ethel, a woman who had hopes, wishes, dreams, relationships, and needs that were separate and distinct from her parental role for me.

It wasn't a big moment—she had come to Chicago, stopped by my place to bring me a gift and take me to lunch, then left to visit her sisters for the weekend. I didn't see or hear from her again until she called to check in before she flew back home to Louisiana. That was the first time ever being in the same city that her plans and activities didn't revolve around me. At first, I was hurt they didn't include me but when I heard the joy in her voice after her weekend with my aunts—especially so soon after the loss of another—I realized that trip and their relationship had nothing to do with her role as my mother, or with me. She needed something from that relationship, which existed long before I ever came around. I was enough of an adult by then that I could step back and fully appreciate that, up until that point, I had only seen her through her role in my life and what she provided for me. Because I was growing up, changing, learning about myself, and becoming more independent of her, I was better able to step back from her and to see her more fully and clearly. It was like my image of her went from black and white to color, HD to 4K.

This happened long before I named and fully understood what *Fearless Authenticity* was, but looking back, having that experience contributed to its development, especially in building relationships—having a fuller understanding of ourselves helps us understand and appreciate others for who they truly are, separate from the roles they fill in our lives. It's easy to love the role others fill in our life. But how do we feel about them beyond that? If they no longer filled that role, what would they mean to us? Not conflating the two deepens the quality of the relationship.

Like I did with my mom, when you're a child, you see your parent as the parent and that's it. That's not an identity or person, it's just a role. Now that role can absolutely be part of your identity, but it's not all of who you are. You don't come out of the womb into this world as a parent. You may be meant to be one; you may be an amazing parent and great with kids, but you had a whole life before that, along with hopes and dreams that didn't necessarily have anything to do with parenthood. A lot of times—especially for us as women, but all genders can experience it—once people become parents, that's the only dimension of their identity that anyone sees, from their children to those in the world around them.

This all hit home for me when I was caring for my dad after his dementia diagnosis. I've seen it happen to every last one of my friends, too, as they tended to their mothers and fathers through illnesses. It is extraordinarily difficult to transition from being the child to parenting your parents because it requires you to see beyond the parent–child relationship, even if you have already experienced them as adults. When your parent gets sick, all of a sudden, everything shifts and you realize, *Oh, this isn't about me as the child anymore. At all.*

I see it as a microcosm of *Fearless Authenticity*: First, we have our own identity—I'm Jeanne. Then we experience the process of peeling back the layers of who our parents are, outside their relationship to us—she's not just Mama, she's Ethel, or he's not just Daddy, he's Allen. And as those parental roles fall away, we see the full human inside. That's where we add to our identity and assume a new role ourselves.

I remember one time Daddy trying to explain to me how he thought his condition might've been caused by a head injury he suffered at work. Or because he was exposed to asbestos on the job or injuries he'd sustained as a child. He was really grappling with what it could be, because his facility with language was failing him, and he couldn't fully express what he was experiencing. He wanted to have a reason for it all. I told him it could be any one of those things, but the question I had was, does it really matter? Even if we did know, would it actually make a difference in that moment? I'm not a parent, but I remember having those moments as a teen where he and my mama said the same types of things to me to help me move forward when I got stuck. And I sure felt like a parent when I had to say it to him in this situation.

That was a pivotal moment for me—I understood that I was now the caregiver. I was now responsible for him instead of the other way around. My role had changed in our relationship and I had to relearn how to connect with him from everything that role represents. I was blessed that Daddy always remembered who I was throughout his cognitive decline, unlike some of my friends who had to reintroduce themselves to their parents each time they met. Still, we had to navigate how to redefine and rebuild our relationship. Looking back on it, that was a bigger challenge for me than the disease itself . . . and maybe it was the same for him, too.

What got me through that experience was focusing on the process that *Fearless Authenticity* gave me to approach it: knowing who I was and where I was in relation to him at all times. I had to be open to meeting somebody new inside my father, this person I loved, every single time I saw him, and seeing how I could connect with this new person and serve his new and ever-changing needs. I fell short many times, and he still parented me through those moments, going back to who he was to me originally and what our relationship once was. The entire time he lived with dementia was a delicate dance of him surrendering past authority and independence for much-needed help, and me giving him that help while giving up being Spro's Baby Girl. That experience also served as a constant reminder for me that even though we often think people with dementia are "gone," they're very much still here.

One particular incident stands out when I felt like I really let him down: We had gone to the grocery store after a long day of appointments. I had wanted to drop him at home so I could get the shopping done quickly, but he insisted on coming along. At the store, he kept grabbing crazy stuff off the shelves, food he wasn't supposed to eat. They were all things his doctor had warned me he might get cravings for and that I might not win that battle. At first, I was frustrated, but I just gave up and let him get what he wanted. When we got home, he was trying to help me put the groceries away, but he wasn't really—there was no rhyme or reason to any of it. I told him to sit down and watch TV and just let me do it. But he ignored me, so again, I let him do it, but I would go behind him and move it to where it should be. He eventually got fed up with that and left. I got everything done quickly after that, but, man, did I feel bad.

When he came back a little while later, he was ready to eat. So, I fixed him a plate and he sat down, patted the table, trying to get me to sit down with him and eat, too. I said, "Daddy, I'm not hungry," in a sharper tone than necessary.

"Okay," he said calmly and continued eating. In that moment, I recognized my dad was parenting me, even through his challenges, and I was not working with him, and that just about broke me down. I was done with everything, and I decided to leave so he wouldn't think I was upset with him, but he clearly understood what was going on and he looked at me with concern.

That's when the dam broke. "Daddy, I'm sorry," I said as the tears started falling. He hugged me and kissed me on the forehead like he did when I was little and upset. I thought to myself, *Good God, this man's brain is disintegrating in front of me, and he's still the bigger person,* and that's when I knew for sure he was still in there. It's hard to remember that when you're in the middle of it.

The *Fearless Authenticity* lesson for me through all of this change was staying present in the moment and being intentional with everything I did. Or at least trying to. *Fearless Authenticity* was the guide to being solid and clear about who I was and how that was changing, while paying attention to who my father was and how he was changing, then understanding how those changes shifted the way we shared information, told each other stories, and served each other's needs. My experience as my daddy's caregiver taught me how to walk it like I talk it. It was yet another moment in my life that I realized *Fearless Authenticity* wasn't just something for me to share with others to use at work—it was also my lesson to learn in this life.

The experience I gained putting it to use in that situation gave me further insights into how my Foundations for Success—especially *Sell It*—work and evolve in our everyday relationships. The questions I was asking myself about my dad had changed to:

- Who is he *now?*

- What does he care about *now?*

- How can I serve him *now?*

If that's not what caregiving is all about, I don't know what is.

And those questions go far beyond caring for our parents or in relationships with other adults. You can also ask those same questions as a parent to young children in navigating all the changes they'll go through. Heidi Stevens told me she had to let go of her expectations for her two kids and reassess what they really needed when she was going through her divorce.

"My kids were two and six, which is little, to be a single mom. I was wondering if I was doing the right thing by breaking my family apart—it was my decision to leave. Then it was just the three of us . . . I definitely made a ton of mistakes. I think the kernel of wisdom I would try to learn sooner if I could go back and do it again . . . is that I needed to let go of giving my kids what I had and what I imagined them having, which was two parents together and an intact family."

When she accepted that their childhood would be very different, she was able to let go and serve them. "It doesn't need to look like mine, it needs to look like the best theirs can be, and I decided I wanted it to be filled with joy . . . that's the one thing we're gonna go for. So, we didn't do a lot of bedtime or chores or sort of like standard things that I think you would try to instill in two- and six-year-olds. . . . We jumped on the bed or we did bike rides to Dairy Queen way too late in the night, or [got] a pink Christmas tree."

Heidi said that, despite the difficulties, she's grateful for how things turned out. "It was probably the hardest time in my life just sort of logistically and financially . . . and it was also honestly one of the sweetest. We were just like this little trio, figuring it out. And it made us really close."

Heidi's ability to let go of understanding how she would impact her children's lives if she pushed to give them what they ultimately couldn't have allowed her to give space to whatever the future actually held for them. That's where the *Tell It* part of the Foundations for Success comes into play. You can't create the story individually, at least not successfully. The story is something you create together.

That collectivity is not always obvious to parents because of the way their generation was raised and assumptions they've made about what they're supposed to be doing as parents and the way things should be. I was surprised in one of my early *Fearless Authenticity* client training sessions when I was explaining that everyone has an audience, and a parent exclaimed, "I'm going home and using this shit on my kids!" Everybody laughed but it set off light bulbs in the heads of the other parents in the room who realized they could use it to get things done around the house. All of them said they'd never thought of their children as an audience, much less serving their children or figuring out what they need to hear in any given moment. One single mother said she hadn't thought to consider what her son needed to find motivation. I repeated what I tell anyone in a one-on-one situation—that even though it was just the two of them, she still had an audience of one. I had no idea before that moment how *Fearless Authenticity* concepts might apply to families.

The same shift in relationship dynamics to collectivity and co-creation can happen in all other kinds of relationships, whether they're friendships, work relationships, or romantic partnerships. As you get to know yourself better, you're better able to meet others exactly where they are—and beyond the role they may play in your life and all the assumptions that come with them. You're also not looking for validation through someone else creating the whole story of the relationship. You take on your share of the responsibility and grasp that *I'm creating something with another person who has needs the same way I have needs.* So, instead of being all about our expectations and what we can get, relationships then become an exchange where we see and engage with all sides of another person, rather than only the role that person might fill in our lives. When we do that, we can enter relationships with others more honestly and holistically without preconceived notions or judgments.

Those preconceived notions or judgments often derail our relationships before they even begin. Take, for example, what happens when you meet someone new: There are times you dislike them on sight. Something just rubs you the wrong way about them. But the next time you encounter them, you have the opposite experience and can't remember for the life of you why you couldn't stand them before. It could be about them and how they were showing up in that moment. Maybe they were trying to impress you or someone else in the room, and their behavior didn't ring true for you and turned you off.

Another possibility is how you mesh—or don't. Maybe the first time you met, you were in mindsets or at points in your lives that went together like oil and water. Perhaps the second time around, something shifted for you and/or them in the time that passed, and you saw each other in a different way. Or maybe you just opened your eyes and realized you had been determined to see them in a way that wasn't accurate.

Let me take you back to high school, where this happened to me and probably happened to you, too, because every high school in every generation has had cliques, and we all participated in them in some way. So, in my version of this story, I started out avoiding (and judging) a group of girls just because my friends actively disliked them. (Pretty sure it had something to do with boys, clothes, or some other such nonsense that was so important at the time. Sound familiar?) Later I was with that group of girls away from my friends. As we talked, I discovered all these things we had in common. I also realized they had no idea my friends felt the way they did. After that, my friendships shifted. I felt so dumb, because I had been judging these girls solely based on what other people were saying about them, not anything I knew to be true from my own experience, and I had missed out on that friendship all that time. Now, there may still have been entirely valid reasons why individuals in the first group of friends didn't mesh with those from the second group, but what I learned from all this is that other people's truths don't define my experience—I'm the only one who can decide who my people are.

Sharing our experiences in interactions with others with our groups can protect us from potential harm, but when it goes to the extreme of groupthink with no space for individual variance, it pushes us further away from choosing for ourselves, which is just another way of chipping away at our *Fearless Authenticity*. And in terms of relationships, especially related to our work, limiting those connections also limits our experiences and opportunities for fulfilling our purpose. As much as we'd like to think all that ended in high school, this is how many of our adult friendships and work relationships still function, unless we choose differently.

So, what does choosing differently—and authentically—for yourself look like? A whole lot like it did when I navigated my changing relationship with my father—knowing who you are and/or are becoming, remaining open to the possibilities you'll encounter in the other person, staying present so you can really listen, and recognizing what's happening and respond. Easier said than done, I know. Being present means first acknowledging that you do not know everything that's happening with the other person. That's how you let go of your expectations of them. Once you do that, then you are much more able to start your discovery process, which begins with "Let me listen." I suggest using a crisis communication management model:

1. *Hear the question.* Listen to the question itself and everything that it's made of—the words used, the emotions expressed, and most importantly, what's implied or left unsaid. That last part is the most challenging because mutual understanding may be assumed or it could be something that's too hard to say out loud, like the proverbial elephant in the room that everyone sees but won't acknowledge. Understanding this is what's at the core of the questions we ask about our audience in "*Sell It*" in chapter 6, especially what they care about. When we know that, or get close to knowing that, we can put ourselves in their shoes; it's the oral communication equivalent of reading between the lines.

My Northwestern colleague Dr. Kimberly Pusateri calls it "generous listening." She specializes in health communication, where generous listening can make all the difference in a patient's treatment plan and outcomes, just from the way their providers understand what they're saying. That's become one of my favorite terms since she introduced it to me, because of the grace it gives both sides of the question.

2. *Acknowledge the question.* Repeat back what you've heard. We all want to be heard and this is a healthy first step to doing that—and you'd be surprised how many people feel like no one hears what they're asking, much less saying. Also find a way to tactfully incorporate those things that you think may have been implied or left unsaid. Sometimes, it's as simple as restating the question in your own words or even repeating the question back verbatim if you can: "If I'm understanding you correctly, you'd like to know why the sky is blue and how I feel about that?" That gives the asker the opportunity to correct or clarify. Getting agreement on what question you're answering also keeps everyone on the same page.

3. *Answer the question to the best of my ability (and also make my point).* Keep it simple when answering any question. People can only take in so much at a time. And remember, "I don't know" is also an answer. If that's the case, it does help if you can follow it up with, "I can find out from X person by Y

time," and if you have anything to share that might add to their understanding. Pay attention to how your answer is being received—that will give you cues on what to do in the next step.

4. *Move forward.* This is the point in an actual crisis communication that most people refer to as the pivot, where you can either guide the line of questioning back to safer ground and/or redirect to the information you want those listening to remember most. It's also the step most want to skip to right after the question is asked, never even acknowledging it. (We see politicians and spokespersons do this all the time with differing results—that approach would probably take a whole other book to break down!) I suggest using this as an opportunity to keep the dialogue open or find resolution.

When you listen first as a habit, all your relationships will get better, simply because you have more information. Some relationships might end, too, because that information will help you discern when it's run its course and/or served its purpose. But at least things get clearer. It also has something to do with releasing those expectations, taking some responsibility yourself, and not projecting your shit or making it someone else's fault, which is what we do when we don't want to face how we've participated in creating our own pain. I'll leave that part to you and your therapist.

This approach to listening is just one part of it. Another part is getting out of our heads and out of our own way. All of us make that mistake at some point; it's how we lose our way in relationships. One of the biggest oversights we make when we have something to say is forgetting that there's more to it than just what's coming out of our mouths. Every communication is an exchange, a two-way street. But we often treat them as announcements, where all that matters is getting our words out. Our worst arguments happen this way, when each person is just waiting for the other to stop talking so they can get their point in (or get that lick back), which gets us nowhere—except maybe to a breakup. A true exchange serves us and the other person, and that only happens when we focus on what the situation requires and fully consider what the person listening needs but may not be getting. When we serve that, we take advantage of an opportunity to create connections in new situations or strengthen bonds with those we already know.

That's exemplified in that saying we've all heard—we've got two ears and one mouth, so we should listen twice as much as we speak. Many of us struggle with that; others have mastered it and it shows. Jon Harris is one of those masters, and his story illustrates how our personal lessons that lead to discovering our *Fearless Authenticity* also lead to success. Jon, the chief communications and networking officer at Conagra Brands, learned to listen at a very young age. He developed his generous communication skills in response to his difficult home life. His father was mentally ill, so he spent his youth helping care for his mother and two younger brothers.

"I was the man of the house even before my father passed [when Jon was nineteen]. I had a lot of those responsibilities," he said. "So, I had a great sense of empathy and [commitment] to be empathetic toward others. What I learned at the time was I always want to help people. My goal is to be a connector. . . . I've always wanted to help people, because I knew what it was like to not have anyone. . . . I learned early on in my life that the time to make friends is not when you need them, but always."

His wisdom in building durable, authentic relationships extends to another reason they're worth the effort: "True relationships with people . . . are only achieved when it's face-to-face . . . when it's nurturing . . . the real relationships, the ones that mean the most to you, are the ones that you're constantly nurturing throughout life. . . . We are really only as good as the friends that we keep in life."

Our relationships clearly have a positive impact on our personal lives and development, but so many of us don't bring them to our work. Emily Chang, author of *The Spare Room* and CEO of Wunderman Thompson, West Coast Region, once firmly believed in keeping her work and home life separate. Then, a simple but key question from a long-ago office visitor forever changed her perspective—and transformed her leadership style.

"A friend [now] named William Travis . . . was trying to sell me something. I was the chief commercial officer at IHG . . . and at the end of the meeting, he's like, 'Thank you for your time,' and then he peeked around the corner of my office and saw this wall . . . and he saw all these photos of all these kids. And he said, 'Can I just ask you who those kids are?' We started talking. . . . We kind of related as humans . . . and he kind of saw the humanity in me. He said, 'Why do you keep those two things separate? I'm just asking.' I said that really has nothing to do with work. And in retrospect that moment changed me; it changed the way I approach work with fearless authenticity, of bringing my life and my vulnerability and my kids at home and everything we do as a family into the workplace . . . and now, years later, I reflect and say I'm such a better person and hopefully a better leader because of it."

So often, we bifurcate our lives into work and personal. As I've mentioned, when I first started in radio and then TV, I kept my private life private. No sharing of romantic partners and very little about my family. Then, after working with Melissa and talking with Glennon Doyle, I realized how vulnerability in one area serves the other and how they're both part of one living, breathing organism that, when integrated, can lead to greater success. When you share authentically and with vulnerability, it's returned in kind. It feeds itself and others feed off it as well. It's just like that saying, "What you put out, you get back."

To improve the flow between our work and personal lives, Emily wants to do away with the concept of work-life balance. "Structurally, it doesn't make sense. Balance is a near impossibility. . . . Instead of trying to balance two things where all our attention and resources are invested in trying to maintain this balance, we put it together and deal with more of this messy middle that, together, might look different for everybody. But if we integrate work and family, I think we live differently, we engage differently, and we lead differently."

When she pursued more of that messy middle, Emily felt less like a boss and more like a leader. "When people can see you as human, you take a lot of that friction away, you just kind of grease it. . . . It brings out the very best with your teams, because they see you as human, not just the boss. The boss as a label is so hard to overcome. It's a wall. It's not that I'm not the boss, but I want to be more than that. I want to be a leader who's in front and breaking down barriers for you. I want to be at your side, rolling up my sleeves, helping when I need to. And I would love the privilege of being behind you and pushing you into the spotlight."

Doing that requires revealing our human side, which Emily believes is worth the risk. "When I'm willing to be vulnerable, if I'm willing to show people I'm hurting or insecure or feeling like I'm failing, what does that put me in? Does it make me suddenly 'the weak woman who doesn't deserve her job' genre? . . . It's a choice I made a while ago to say I'm going to be okay with my emotions. I think I'm going to show them to my teams and I think it'll help take down that wall, but it will help them feel like they can be more real with me. . . . We have to be the ones who are fearless and equally willing to be vulnerable—setting the stage, showing the example—before others might feel free to do the same."

Taking ownership of your stuff, your emotions and where you're at—at work, at home, or anywhere else—fits into my first Foundation for Success—*Live It*. This is where the culture of your company, team, family, or friend story begins. Being your authentic self starts the ball rolling. After that, others will follow your lead. Then it's about deciding with the second Foundation, *Tell It*, what kind of bridge you're going to build through stories to make connections and find your purpose. And pulling it all together by relying on Foundation number three, *Sell It*, to understand what the people you're sharing all that with, your audience, cares about and how you can serve them now. And you can do that literally anywhere with anyone. I have yet to find a place where it doesn't apply.

Many of my clients who come to me for help with their professional communication skills soon understand that revealing their *Fearless Authenticity* at home with the help of my Foundations for Success helps them better navigate their personal relationships. Applying *Live It, Tell It, Sell It* to more than work makes sense because even though the average person will spend ninety thousand hours at work over a lifetime (according to industrial-organizational psychologist and data scientist Andrew Naber), there are relationships embedded in work that have nothing to do with the work you're trying to accomplish together. Even though we try to compartmentalize stuff, our work leaks into our family or personal life. The confidence we get from doing well at work affects our personal lives, especially romantic relationships. The converse is true as well—if your house is not in order, you bring some of those issues with you to the office.

Emily summed up beautifully why *Fearless Authenticity* is so important in our everyday lives: "Authenticity requires a degree of vulnerability, and also of humility. And it's not easy to remain grounded in humility. So, it does take a degree of fearlessness. I think if we aren't fearless, we can't get to that stage of true, completely unmasked authenticity . . . the kind that helps people . . . see each other and feel that flame and be like, 'Yes, this is one of my people.'"

BE BRAVE
AUTHENTICITY ACTION

A thought exercise for you:

1. How do you argue with integrity and disagree with authenticity in your relationships?

2. What do you choose to share or not with your family about your work life? And why?

3. What do you choose to share (or not) with your colleagues about yourself as a person outside of the work you do together? And why?

CHAPTER 10

Living in Your Fearless Authenticity

earless Authenticity is a journey—but I think you've figured that out by now! Learning to live as your authentic self is a lifelong exploration, and it's one that I'm still on myself, so we're in this together. If we're doing it right, that looks like meeting every moment as it comes, choosing to respond in ways that best reflect who we are, how we feel, and how we want to engage with the world around us. With every choice, we uncover layers of ourselves we haven't met before but were always there, create new aspects that help us get closer to the person we're meant to become and want to be, and get closer to fulfilling our purpose on this planet, personally and professionally, step by *Fearlessly Authentic* step.

Looking back over my authenticity odyssey so far, of course, it started with my parents seeing me, choosing me, and laying the foundation to support who I would become. I've moved forward—sometimes pushed, other times pulled—thanks to help from some incredible people who have left indelible marks on my life, encouraging me to make fearless choices so I could find and hone my gifts along the way. But it took getting to midlife and surviving some bumps in the road to look back and see how each step led to where I am now.

Over the course of my career, I've interviewed thousands of people, and one of the questions I've been most interested in is their turning point—the moment in their lives that set them on the path to where they are now, the moment they knew that they were doing what they were meant to do. My consistent curiosity about that is because, for the longest time, I wasn't able to see what my turning point was, and I wanted to know what that looked and felt like to see if I'd actually had one. It's only been through writing this book that I could see—no matter how clear it may have been to others—that my early years in radio were the moment I started to understand how to be and become my best, truest self.

I had the absolute privilege of working with comedy legend George Wallace as well as the four men highlighted in the Spike Lee film *The Original Kings of Comedy*— Steve Harvey, Bernie Mac, Cedric the Entertainer, and D. L. Hughley. They were my mentors, exemplars, and inspiration while I was on the air at WGCI-FM in Chicago in the mid-nineties. I cohosted mornings with both George and Steve while the other guys would fill in pretty frequently.

From those brilliant, generous men, I saw what it took for them to get to where they were. I gained insight into what I needed to do to use the environment I was in to get to where I wanted to be, to express myself and build my audience, fearlessly. Bernie, in particular, really sparked something in my development. His approach to comedy was essentially playing a mind game with the audience, and maybe himself. You know his signature phrase: "I ain't scared of you!"

When someone walks onstage saying that, it brings an entirely different energy and attitude to the party, laying down the line and essentially saying, "This is who I am, and I couldn't give two f's about what you think about it, you hear?"

It's bold, it's brash, it's a bona fide commitment to who you are. Bernie was absolutely fearless onstage and in life, and that unabashed mindset stuck with me as I got to know him.

One time when he filled in for Steve, he asked me, "Where do you usually sit?"

I said, "Well, right here. Steve usually stands over there."

Bernie rolled his eyes about Steve standing and then told me, "Get up, Jeanne."

"For what?" I asked.

"I'm you today," he said, "and you are Steve. I'm gonna do what you tell me to do. I ain't trying to have no radio show. I'm not trying to replace Steve or you. I've been listening; you've been holding down this shit while he is gone. So, I'ma help you do it. If your boss don't think you're good enough to do it, well, fine. Fuck him. And that's how we're gonna do it today."

Being with superstars like them at that stage of my career was just what I needed. Bernie, George, Steve, and every single comic I worked with set me on my then-unknown, unaware mission to find my *Fearless Authenticity*. What they did helped me understand what I did; what my role was; what purpose I served; and how I could work inside this box and push it out to create my own box. It also gave me a certain amount of discipline about what my work needed to look like, how I needed to prepare, what I needed to do, what kind of impact I wanted to have, how I wanted my audience to feel.

When I moved on to television, the same feelings I'd had when I was starting in radio returned—that I had to be perfect. But my experience with those uninhibited veteran performers gave me the confidence to know what I needed to do to work it out. I needed to exercise that TV muscle, just like they did when they were working out new material onstage:

"We don't always know what we're doing or how it's going to turn out," is what their work said to me. "But we're gonna do it anyway because there's no other way to do it. You can't fake it. You can't work out what you do well until you do it."

At some point, you would think that if you work it out long enough, you'll get to the optimal expression of yourself. But nope, you won't. Why? Because as you uncover all your layers, you realize you're still getting to know yourself and discovering what you have to say, do, be. *Your life is all about getting to know you.* As you do that, you'll discover new things and take some left turns that you did not expect.

Brett Berish, entrepreneur, president, and CEO of Sovereign Brands, knows all about left turns. Although his family has been in the beverage industry for decades, he didn't join in until he was in his thirties. "I was late in life doing this," he said. "I was lost for years. I tell everybody this: 'There's just some people who know what they want to be when they grow up. I didn't know.' I had too many ideas. I was always afraid of picking one because I figured that was the wrong idea. And what happens if that's the wrong one?"

Picking the wrong one is part of the *Fearless Authenticity* process, the peeling back of your onion, so to speak. A friend who's a therapist said even he had a moment when he realized, "Oh, every time I unpeel a piece of this onion (myself), there's yet another piece to go and they're all going to make me cry." Or in another strangely fitting vegetable analogy, when I was first learning to cook with my mama, I was cutting up some celery and trying to strip off the strings that were dangling.

"Baby, don't even bother," Mama said.

"Don't bother with what?" I asked.

"Don't try to take the strings off celery," she explained. "When I first started cooking, I tried to take the strings off, too, because I hated how they got caught in my teeth, and then I finally realized the whole thing is nothing but strings. The more strings you pull off, the more strings there are. You just got to let them be and chop it all up."

Though she meant it in a very literal sense at the time, it also works as a metaphor for all that we are. When we look at ourselves as a whole, the strings don't show. But after you notice and tug at one, you start to see them all as part of the whole. And once you know you're made of all those strings, why would you ever try to get rid of them? You couldn't if you tried. And if you succeeded, there would be nothing left. Your strings are all your successes, along with all your failures and every other half-assed, half-baked thing you've tried and done. Seeing them is seeing ourselves, each part of us, as we grow and learn about ourselves and eventually how we find the reward in our struggles. In my experience and what I've seen with my clients, every time we follow one of those threads, we discover something we haven't shared, unlock something we didn't know about ourselves, or find something in need of healing that promotes our pain into wisdom. And there's always a blessing right on the other side of all that.

Brett has had a couple of those moments over the years. The first was when he finally decided to join the family business. He realized he no longer cared what anyone else thought about his choice and he would do what it is he wanted to do. His choice clearly paid off—his portfolio of wine and spirits is now a global phenomenon, known for its unique premium brands and celebrity partnerships.

His second moment of clarity came about six years into running his company. His investors had lost faith in him and wanted to blow it all up. It took his mother offering to sell her jewelry to help keep him in business for Brett to realize how fully committed he was to making it work.

"I loved what I was doing. It isn't about the money anymore. If I could just survive, I'd be happy. And at that moment, it just slowed down. It's not about how quickly you get there. It's about having patience and eventually you'll get there. Some people are lucky. It happens really quick. For others, it takes a long time. But if you love what you're doing, and it sounds corny, it's real. If you love it . . . just don't worry about it."

That rings true for Tracy Clark, too. As I mentioned earlier, the award-winning Chicago crime writer spent more than twenty years crafting PI novels before ever getting her first book contract.

"Nobody would take it," she shared. "Rejection after rejection . . . that's where the pigheadedness comes in . . .

they wanted to kill me . . . they were trying to make me stop. And there was no way in heck I was gonna."

So many of us face rejection and accept it as the final word. Even if we keep trying, even if we're persistent, there's a little piece of us that still wonders if that rejection was right and maybe we've been fooling ourselves all along and should just give up. Tracy admits to having a moment like that. "I put the book away . . . in a drawer for two years. I didn't touch it . . . I sort of had the decision: it's just not for me, I'm not going to make it, it's too hard. But there was something in here; a little fire right at the heart of me that said: *No, I know you can do this. I know I have something.* But it was also hard, because I knew I would have to start all over again."

This is where knowing who you are comes in—understanding your true self and what you offer to the world. Tracy has wanted to be a writer since she was eight years old; at fifteen, she knew mysteries would be her calling. And she was determined to make her character for *her*: "I didn't want my character to be a sassy sidekick. I didn't want her to be the gum-chewing and headshaking afterthought. I wanted my female African American character to be the main show. I got here now; it took me this long to get here. Tell me to leave and I'm not going."

To help you get to Tracy's rock-solid level of living in her *Fearless Authenticity*, ask yourself these three questions:

1. What do I know that is true about myself in this moment?
2. Having that knowledge about myself, how do I want to engage with others?

3.   Having that knowledge about myself, are there ways
     I choose not to engage with others?

That last question really is the key. It shows your boundary between what serves the situation of others and what
serves you. It's the conversation you have with yourself:
"Okay, this is who I am, what I need, and what I have to offer
here. And that is what the situation is, and what it has to
offer me. Now, I'm choosing to do this and not that because
it serves this situation's and my own highest, greatest good."
That's where you develop a finer understanding and awareness of where you belong and where you don't, and what
challenges are worth fighting through because they bring
you closer to your purpose . . . versus the experiences that
hold nothing of value for you and just drag you down. It's
about being very intentional and present in a way that goes
beyond just an awareness of "I'm in this moment," to the
discernment that says: "I see what's really happening here. I
know what I'm here for, and I'm making a choice to participate in it, for myself and for others."

That includes the awareness of knowing when you're
not quite there yet and saying to yourself, "Okay, I'm putting this load down for a bit and I'll come back when I
have the energy to pick it up again." I can't tell you how
many times I've done that with this book over the years
because I've lost track to get to this last chapter. But every
time it called me back, I had to reexamine it, see what I
did that was great (and not so great), and decide again
if it was time to pick it up or leave it alone to marinate,
because I wasn't ready to take it on. And maybe it wasn't
ready either.

Brett believes that the ability to accept your advantages and limitations is empowering. "Knowing who you are and accepting who you are—that's half the battle. To me, half my battle is owning up to what I am and what I'm not and just trusting that. I think that's what entrepreneurs are and you've got to trust that."

Part of that trust comes from knowing your value, your purpose, and how you're serving that moment. Who's benefiting from this? Why do I care about this? What is my connection? How can I be a vehicle for this? That is how you understand your gift that nobody else can provide. It not only can change moment to moment, it will likely also change across time, and as you commit to this as a regular practice, you'll continually discover these new little nuggets of truth that divulge both your strengths and shortcomings. Sometimes other people will see them and call them to your attention. When your discernment kicks in, you'll know when they're right. You can acknowledge your blind spots and confront your insecurities, which many times camouflage the very thing you excel at.

There's no hiding Lindsay McDonell's deep connection to what is now her life's work and, frankly, full-on passion. She became a cancer coach after her own terminal diagnosis (nearly ten years ago at the time of this publishing) to support other patients through their journey.

"I saw the way that I handled it," she said, "and I knew that I could bring support to other people. . . . Being a cancer coach is my absolute favorite thing to do in the world. It's a hard place to be, but there is so much joy you can find in it as well . . . and people don't really look at it that way."

Fearless Authenticity plays right into Lindsay's coaching philosophy. "The role you want people to get to is to be able to deal with this from their authentic center. . . . What I coach in all of them is not to live out of fear. Because if you're living out of fear, your curiosity is going to be completely crushed, and if your curiosity is crushed, then the joy of life is gonna go right out. They need to be able to regain some of the control and power that they felt in life. But now, not from an ego standpoint, from their heart. Because from there, you're going to go further."

At the core of *Fearless Authenticity* is knowing yourself well and engaging in the process of developing it from that knowledge—whether you're trying to make an improvement, change something you don't like, accept something you can't change, or just work with all of who you are. We don't always like ourselves or certain things about ourselves. The beautiful thing about *Fearless Authenticity* is we can always shift how we feel about our authenticity. That's how we discover its advantages and see it as the gift it is.

For Lindsay's own cancer journey, she knew no tools she had from her previous life as an interior designer could help her keep cancer at bay.

"I had to learn to let go . . . to reach deeper into the tool kit and find another path at which I was able to do the fearlessness part and authenticity. . . . A good portion of us are living out how we want people to see us rather than how we are. From that position, unfortunately, your authentic self gets hidden and people see what you want them to see, maybe . . . because without your authenticity, what they're seeing, you may think you want them to see, but you need that little extra piece in there that's really you. . . . What I teach people is how to get back to who they are and to stop listening to their whole world telling them what to do."

We often equate success with what we think others want, when in reality, true success comes when we move with authenticity—it's easy, natural, and empowering. One way to feel that empowerment is through self-care—two of my favorite words. The better we take care of ourselves, the better we can show up in the world in whatever we do, whether it's for the people we love, for our work, or for our health, as in Lindsay's case.

"Whether it's meditation or journaling or community," she told me, "whatever the things are that support you in the world, to really put a bead on that. . . . Honestly we can all do it. Because all of those things are meant to bring you back to your center, and from your center, there's enormous power there."

Fearless Authenticity is how you focus that power in your daily life. It's a vehicle to know yourself so well and commit so deeply to what you do well that you find success through it. Not through the ways other people say it should be done, even though it's still done in service to those same people. That's what self-awareness is all about.

Rebecca Sive's deep commitment to women's rights and civil rights spans more than fifty years. Her devotion to public policy and government began at the age of eight when she joined her father in his campaign for Congress.

"There's never been a moment, in all seriousness," she told me, "when these were not joined for me. The notion of civil rights, particularly for African Americans in the US, and women's rights here as well. My parents taught us that everybody was equal. . . . I grew up with the notion that the Declaration of Independence should be really true for everybody."

To that end, she has written three books on American women's politics and power, is a speaker and nationally respected strategist on women's leadership, was a founding member of the Illinois Human Rights Commission, and an advisor to many history makers, including Chicago's first African American mayor, Harold Washington, former presidents Bill Clinton and Barack Obama, Michelle Obama, Geraldine Ferraro, and many others.

What has sustained Rebecca's dedication is her drive to bring people together. "Contrary to what some may think . . . there are some of us who have been working specifically together across racial lines for a very long time."

And while she acknowledges there is profound systemic racism and sexism in our country now, there's been forward movement over time. "There were goals that I and my sisters of my generation had that were not achieved by women of earlier generations . . . and in order to get there, we had to not fear success . . . [or] what we needed to be successful, which was [being] assertive."

Helping women tell their success stories is part of who Rebecca is. "Everybody, every person, every woman has the power within herself, the intelligence, the fortitude, the grit, to be somebody. To contribute to the common good, and to achieve for herself . . . once you identify your story, once you can imagine it, then you can go about the business of creating it, of organizing it, of doing it."

And while Rebecca's work is directed toward public life, her strategies can work for anyone. It all comes down to what we should already know if we're really living in our *Fearless Authenticity* like she is.

"It's knowing one's own story . . . that it isn't the sort of litany of 'I went to this school or that school.' It's who am I, right? Who am I? And therefore, what can I then take from who I am to then build this career."

For Shaka Rawls, however, his story *is* all about the school he went to and now leads. He's the principal of Leo High School, a private all-male Catholic high school on the South Side of Chicago and his alma mater. He told me he believes he's doing what God put him on Earth to do, which is, of course, what *Fearless Authenticity* is all about. His approach to education focuses on bringing out the best in his students and ensuring they never doubt their worth.

"I trade in the most expensive commerce there is—I trade in love. I am here every day giving 100 percent to these boys and expecting 100 percent from them. If you know anything about teenage boys, they're not going to give you 100 percent every day. So, that means every evening I'm disappointed. . . . I desire to be my best for these boys every single day and when I see that I'm not, it hurts. I go home and cry. . . . I am emotionally exhausted every single day. I laugh in this building, I cry, I yell, I smile. I have all these emotions every single day—that's why I love this job."

Shaka proves my assertion that *Fearless Authenticity* is as much for other people as it is for yourself. There are some who will hear *Fearless Authenticity* and think it's just about expressing yourself. Others will hear it as, "Oh, I gotta develop my gifts so that I'm marketable." While still others will hear, "Oh, I have to do this in service of others because that's what I'm meant to do."

It's all of those things. It's a holistic approach to how you move through the world and how you find success. Having flexibility is really important. But many people water down what they do best by trying to do everything so they can stay in the loop. Sometimes it's not their choice; it's what they need to do to keep their job, so they do it instead of saying, "How can I make this my own? How can I stay true to who I am and what I'm supposed to be doing?"

Shaka has stayed true to himself by reminding people that there's a person underneath the principal role. "I'm a shepherd of these boys. . . . I only have one gear and it's gonna have to be myself because boys smell BS a mile away. They know when I'm not giving it to them straight. So, I gotta be myself. I gotta stay consistent. . . . I think that just being not afraid to be who you are, whether that's a former kid from Woodlawn Gardens on the South Side of Chicago, or that 'gonna be' PhD student from the University of Chicago. . . . I hit all the corners but I represent both of them spaces 100 percent of any room I walk in." (Shaka is officially Dr. Rawls now!)

Here's where *Fearless Authenticity* becomes a practice. When we are making changes, whether it's anything from improving our health, rising in our career, or earning an education, we have a goal we're working toward. Having that goal suggests in our head that we are going to stop at some point, that there is an end point . . . but no, we have to work on this for the rest of our lives. *Fearless Authenticity* is not something you can just stop working on. There will always be new areas to explore and progress to be made. Shaka is not afraid of the challenge.

"I want the boys to know, even though it's difficult, it's not impossible. It's just hard. . . . I work every Saturday, I work most Sundays, six, seven days a week because I think that we do have a phenomenal product, but it also takes a phenomenal effort to produce that product . . . when you love the grind and you love to see what the progress is and the process, then you understand that it's okay to tell the boys that I love you. It's okay to tell the boys I'm angry with you. But you have to be comfortable enough to withstand students rejecting you wholeheartedly. But also looking at the students, and there's 210 kids in this building, and I'm sure only two hundred of them really love me like I love them. But I'll take that all day. I'm tending to a flock. . . . You have to be able to be really comfortable in yourself to withstand those types of turmoil. And also your heart's gotta be strong enough to endure it."

Endure, indeed. Shaka proves on a daily basis that the more you know, the more you learn, the more you reveal of yourself and your vulnerability—the more you have to show and teach others. And the more you get back.

The more I learn about myself and *Fearless Authenticity*, the more I believe I'm on the path I was meant to walk. That's the gift *Fearless Authenticity* has given me. I spent a good part of my life waiting to feel this way, wondering at each turn if I was making the right choice, pursuing the right goals, doing the right things. What I've discovered is that it was all right, because anything different may not have led me here to my purpose, to *Fearless Authenticity*.

I'm still on my lifelong *Fearless Authenticity* journey—enduring, exploring, learning, and sharing. As I speak about it, train my clients with it, teach it to my students, and write this book, the more it reveals itself to me. In the six-plus years since I first started committing these words to paper,

I've refined it, defended it, answered challenges to it, and used it myself. At every turn, I'm more and more convinced of how durable, adaptable, and useful it is. This concept and process has helped me make sense of everything I've experienced along the way, whether I look forward or back. I've been peaceful and sure of where I'm going, even if I don't know exactly where that is at every moment.

What I hope most of all is that what I've shared in this book will give you a way of thinking about yourself and your gifts and how to put them to use in a way that makes you happier, more successful, more confident, surer of your path, and most of all, whole.

Because that is how you leave your mark on the world.

BE BRAVE, BE FREE, BE YOU
AUTHENTICITY ACTION

We're all a work in progress.

A thought exercise for you.

What have you discovered so far about your true value as you work to better serve yourself and those around you?

ACKNOWLEDGMENTS

To everyone doing your best to live in your truth and use your powers to make the world a better place, thank you. You and what we are creating together are why I do this work.

I salute my ancestors on the Sparrow, Atlas, and Malveaux lines for your perseverance that pushes your future generations to heights beyond your wildest dreams. To my parents, Allen and Ethel, thank you for giving me your best and demanding the best—and the truth—from me. To my biological parents, Mary and Ken, thank you for creating me, giving me the raw materials of my being and having the wisdom to ask others to raise me. To all my cousins, you are my siblings and my compass, especially the Landry sisters, Pam, Nicka, and Nicole.

My chosen family of friends, thank you all for loving me as I am, telling me the truth when I need to be reminded, encouraging me when I'm struggling, celebrating with me when I win, especially Ericka, Melissa, Nika, Grisell, Amy, and Jennifer for listening to me talk about this book for years. Delta love to my sorors for mentoring me, saying my name in rooms I'm not in, and letting me lean on the crest in every way, especially Adrienne, Lori, Michelé, Lucia, Brenda, Carmen, and Bernie. And to my therapist Jinnie Cristerna, thank you for helping me see myself so clearly that I finally got out of my own way.

I once thought writing a book was a solitary pursuit but facing the page is the only part that is. I wouldn't have committed my ideas to paper without the guidance of Sarah Victory—thank you for seeing the book in me that I didn't know was there. It's so much better thanks to the eagle eyes of Cara Smith and Nick Pullia, the moral support of Frank Jones and Rosey Lee, and all the affirmations that Fearless Authenticity is a successful strategy for life from every client who trusted themselves and their teams to this work—especially Christin—and every guest I had on my podcast. And I am forever grateful to my team who lived and breathed this with me: Vicki, Nicole, Lisa E., and Wayne.

To my team at Diversion Books, thank you for helping me finally make this book a reality: Liz Gassman, your enthusiasm and insights helped me weave my ideas and stories into a cohesive whole, and Evan Phail, your clarity, drive, and attention to detail got it done. Special thanks to Casey Embro for your early support and asking the right questions. To my agents: Amy Bishop-Wycisk, thank you for taking the first chance on me, and Michael Bourret, thank you isn't big enough for your diligence, integrity, and sage advice that helped me see this through all the challenges and setbacks when I was almost ready to give it up entirely.

Finally, this book was born through my early career mentors and colleagues who showed me in word and deed how to be fearless and authentic and provided the source material for its foundation: Elroy R. C. Smith, Marv Dyson,

ACKNOWLEDGMENTS

Steve Harvey, the late, great Bernie Mac, and my dear friend and enduring inspiration for how to work and live well, George Wallace.

All honor to the Creator for shining your light through me and every soul in the universe when we choose to let it.